But I Know A God

Encounters, Visitations and Miracles

Dr. Al G. Forniss

Acknowledgements

In memory of my Grandmother Eloise, I honor and thank her for her desire to have me know her God. She prayed for me to serve and sing for the Lord, and it was song which drew me to Him.

I thank my wife Loretta for her deep love and loyal support. Staying at my side through the years of ministry, whether it be in the valley or on the hilltop, always believing the God in me. Also for her unselfishness in lending me to so many.

I thank my three sons, Al Jr., Brandon, and Ryan for sharing me with so many around the world. They taught me the importance to know when to be a pastor and when to be their father.

I thank my daughters-in-love for loving my sons with all their hearts and believing in me as their "Dad" and pastor.

I thank my six grandchildren
Michael, Nicholas, Evan, Christopher, Madison and Jeremy for making me the happiest Grandfather in the world. I also thank them for bestowing on me their personalized name for Grandfather which is
"Peepa".

I give honor to my parents Domingo and Elena who have been instrumental in my life. Thank you for your unwavering love and belief in me.

Last but not least, thank you to all who have helped to see this book find its completion. Special thanks go out to Apostle Rick Kurnow and Pastor Nancy Stern.

CONTENTS

Dear Reader,

I thank you for choosing to read my book. It is the compilation of my experiences with Jesus Christ of Nazareth and the Holy Spirit. My experiences and visitations with Jesus Christ helped to propel my spiritual growth.

Can you believe it? Our precious Father, the God of Abraham, Isaac, and Jacob was actually enlightening my eyes to see beyond my own understanding. This helped to encourage me to not accept less but to always expect more which ultimately began to increase my faith in Him. I understood my life had divine purpose for me as well as for many others. I would eventually understand there was so much more of God that I continued to search for Him but now in a deeper way. Many have asked me how did I search for Him?

I began searching for God through my heartfelt worship to Him keeping my communication constantly focused in prayer and meditation. It was me being still and knowing who He is, was and will always be. I wanted more of His presence; I wanted to touch Him, to feel Him and to see Him. I fell in love with Him. He began to be so real to me. He wasn't a God who was just in heaven sitting on a throne. He was in me, around me and I was His and He was mine. Praise God! I know a living God. He introduced Himself to me as my Savior but in seeking Him I wanted more. That's when I found my precious Lord.

I had sought the Lord telling Him I wanted to have more of Him. I said I wanted to experience His presence and His power. I continued to bring my petition and supplication to Him early in my relationship with Him. After what seemed to me to be an eternity I realized it actually turned out to be only a few months. The Lord gave me instructions directing me to read Ephesians 1:17-23 and also chapter 3:14-21. He told me to make it personal, to change the context and I did. My prayer then read like this:

Ephesians 1:17-23

"*17 that the God of our Lord Jesus Christ, the Father of glory, may give to **me** the spirit of wisdom and revelation in the knowledge of Him, 18 the eyes of **my** understanding being enlightened; that I may know what is the hope of His calling, what are the riches of the glory of His inheritance in **me**, 19 and what is the exceeding greatness of His power toward me who believes, according to the working of His mighty power 20 which He worked in Christ when He raised Him from the dead and seated Him at His right hand in the heavenly places, 21 far above all principality and power and might and dominion, and every name that is named, not only in this age but also in that which is to come. 22 And He put all things under His feet, and gave Him to be head over all things to the church, 23 which is His body, the fullness of Him who fills all in all.*"

Ephesians 3:14-21

"*14 For this reason I bow my knees to the Father of our Lord Jesus Christ, 15 from whom the whole family in heaven and earth is named, 16 that He would grant **me**, according to the riches of His glory, to be strengthened with might through His Spirit in **my** inner man, 17 that Christ may dwell in **my** heart through faith; that I, being rooted and grounded in love, 18 may be able to comprehend with all the saints what is the width and length and depth and height-19 to know the love of Christ which passes knowledge; that I may be filled with all the fullness of God. 20 Now to Him who is able to do exceedingly abundantly above all that I ask or think, according to the power that works in **me**, 21 to Him be glory in the church by Christ Jesus to all generations, forever and ever. Amen.*"

Every night for one year I prayed that prayer. I truly meant business. I wanted to be close to Him and I wanted to know Him. This prayer was the deep calling unto the deep as I learned from *Psalms 42:7*. I began to experience His presence. He began to teach me, reveal Himself to me and at times just commune with me. It was such an intimate time with Him. I was in His Theophany; His tangible and visible presence. I pray my writings will propagate your journey to a higher dimension to discover and personally experience His presence, His love, His intimacy.

Be so overwhelmingly blessed,

Apostle Dr. Al G. Forniss

CHAPTER 1

A PLANE THAT WOULDN'T FLY

This experience was one of the greatest tests which catapulted my faith to a greater dimension in the Father. This story begins when we organized a trip to fly to Canaima National Park in Venezuela. It is the second largest park in the country and the sixth largest park in the world. Angel Falls is found there and it is considered to be the highest falls in the world with an elevation of 3,287 feet. This park is also home to the indigenous Pemon Indians.

I enjoy learning about different cultures, their traditions and their habitats. I appreciate the beauty in the diversity, as well as, in the similarity of each place. I am so grateful to the Lord for allowing me to see His signature and His workmanship He created. When standing at the edge of the Grand Canyon, in Arizona, I could only marvel over the enormity and spans of the canyon and how it offered the most vibrant array of colors which could have only been painted by the hand of God. Seeing the majestic hues of lavender, blue, orange and red painted on the sides of the canyon took my breath away. I experienced God's masterpiece when visiting Costa Rica with its vibrant emerald green jungles. Another place amongst many I have seen was in the city of Cancun, Mexico which offered pristine white sandy beaches and crystal clear turquoise waters. I am always appreciative in experiencing God's beauty.

My wife, Loretta and I along with a group of five associates were so excited to begin our Venezuelan journey. Of all the places we had visited we found each one to be beautiful and unique and we couldn't wait to see what Venezuela offered. As we looked on the map and started to schedule our flights, we noticed other sites we found interesting. We didn't want to miss a thing so we began suggesting other places to visit. We scheduled so many places from Isla de Margarita, a north shore island of Venezuela to Cancun, Belize, and a few more intriguing places. After choosing the ones we wanted to visit, it totaled eleven flights in fourteen days. Wow! I know you might think that's a lot of flying! But what an adventure we were going to have, right?

Loretta and I were so excited with our excursion which was soon coming up. We had only three weeks to get ourselves ready for our trip. Three weeks was not a long time and we had packing, shopping and three boys to tend to.   My yard also needed a facelift which I had promised my wife I would have done before we left.   Making a list of what needed to be done, I wrote down: build a whiskey barrel waterfall, pull out some trees, re-seed the lawn with grass, build planters, plant flowers and small palms, pull weeds and fertilize. I knew this was going to be a lot of work and I had only three weeks in which to finish. I built the three-tier whiskey barrel waterfall, which turned out to not only look nice, but to my surprise it even worked. The lawn after a few weeks began to grow plush and green.

My neighbors would catch me outside and say, "All that hard work paid off, Mr. Forniss." All the plants and flowers were planted and my landscaping job was complete.   I thanked the Lord for His gifts and talents He placed in me. This scripture always resonates in my spirit every time I do something I didn't think I could do, or do well. Philippians 4:13, *"I can do all things through Christ which strengthens me."*

Two days before our date of departure I had, as I now know, a God-given dream. I am always mindful of my dreams and visions because many times God speaks to me through them. Dreams are one of the ways God uses to reveal a message to warn you and/or inform you. Another way is seeing a vision either through my natural eye or with my spiritual eye, which I refer to as my knower. Many times a dream and/or vision can be symbolic or metaphoric. At times both can be given to you allowing you to see places you will be or people you will meet in the future. Through our dreams/visions God speaks to us, He teaches us, He unfolds many crossroads, and cross pollination of people who have been predestined by God to be a part of our purpose and journey.

One of the ways God builds faith is by giving you a dream/vision or an idea deep within your soul which seems unreachable, far beyond your abilities. Something you alone are not capable of doing which requires faith in Him. When God wants to work His purpose in your life He will have you work through it starting with just a dream/vision or idea about yourself, about what He wants you to do, or about how He's going to use your life to impact the world.

There are many examples in the Bible of this.

- God gave Noah a dream of building an ark.

- God gave Abraham a dream of being the father of a great nation.

- God gave Joseph the dream of being a leader that would save his people.

- God gave Nehemiah the dream of rebuilding the wall around Jerusalem

How do we know when a dream/vision or idea is from God or when it's something we've thought up ourselves? The Bible teaches us that God, *"By His mighty power at work within us is able to do far more than we would ever dare to ask or even dream of infinitely beyond our highest prayers, desires, thoughts or hopes…"* (Ephesians 3:20)

In other words, if a dream/vision or idea comes from God, it will be so big in our life we could never do it in our own might or power. If we could do it on our own, we wouldn't need faith. And if we don't have faith we're not pleasing God, because the Bible says, *"For whatever is not from faith is sin."* (Romans 14:23b). God may be speaking to you right now, but you may not have recognized it for what it is. That dream/vision you may have had, that marvelous idea, that over-the-top concept - it's your God given information or instruction download. Yes, God wants to use you. My prayer for you is for the Lord to open your eyes to see, either in a dream/vision or an idea. "Lord, help us to see our journey here on earth. Lord, let your purpose in us be so sure that we can walk in your perfect will. Amen and Amen!"

This is what God gave me, a dream. In this dream I saw I was in a room with a big bay window. I looked out of the window and noticed I saw something I found quite peculiar. There was a long cement walkway which was next to a large pool, next a white wooden gazebo which was close to a marsh like lagoon, a sandy beach, and lastly a blue ocean. In the morning I remembered my dream but thought it was a pizza dream. You know the ones that seem so far-fetched and without meaning. It seemed this dream was just that. I dismissed the dream because it had no relevance to me or of my days to come, but this dream did linger within me leaving me with enough curiosity I shared it with my wife Loretta.

Our day of departure was exciting with packing and planning. My method of packing was to first place everything on the bed I was going to take to help me see if I overlooked anything. I would check and re-check and I would say, "Okay, I'm ready, I didn't miss a thing." But I wasn't fooling myself because like all my other excursions something always was left behind.

We arrived at the airport with passports in hand. We boarded the plane and we were off! Our flight was long with some stopovers but eventually we landed at Isla de Margarita Airport. We were so tired and so in need of showers. We all just wanted to find a comfortable chair or soft bed to fall into but we but first needed to find the shuttle which was prearranged to take us to our hotel. My wife Loretta and I along with our five associates found the shuttle and with luggage in hand we found our seats.

As we approached the entrance of the hotel with its tropical theme we all knew we made a right choice to stay there. I said to myself, "Thank you Jesus our hotel choice was a good one." We stepped out of the shuttle and stretched our legs while being greeted by the staff of the hotel.

The lobby was cool and quite elegant. We had preregistered so our suite and keys were ready and awaiting us. We followed the bellboy, entered our suite and as he placed the luggage in our respective rooms, we found a seat or a bed to fall into. I saw the sofa, fell into it and closed my eyes for a few moments. When I opened my eyes I noticed a big bay window right in front of me and realized it was as if I had seen this window before. God then reminded me of the dream He gave me. I had seen this window in a dream and wondered if what I saw outside in my dream would be there. I walked up to the window, drew the thin loose-knit drapes and didn't see a pool, or walkway, or even the lagoon…well, none of it.

I turned to my wife and said, "This isn't the room we're supposed to be in." I told the others the same thing and they just said, "Pastor, this room will do." They proceeded to try to convince me it didn't matter but I knew they were tired. What could I do but oblige. A few minutes later one of my associate pastors said the phone was not working and the air conditioning in his bedroom was inoperable. It was hot and we absolutely needed our suite to be cooled. I called the front desk and told the attendant of our concerns and he apologized for the inconvenience but told me it was a holiday and the maintenance crew didn't work weekends. He told me the earliest they could repair it would be in two days. I thanked him and hung up the phone and went downstairs to the front desk and asked for the manager. The manager nervously approached me because he knew there was no one at the hotel who would be able to repair the air conditioning. Through his apologies I said, "I know you can't repair the unit but can't you move us to another suite?" He said, "I have a great idea! Let me move you to a new suite. It will be the same but in a different location." I thanked him for *"my"* great idea and walked with him to our suite to tell the others we were relocating.

We gathered our luggage and walked to our new suite. I entered the living room and found myself staring at the bay window. I walked in front of it, drew the drapes and stood there completely astonished of what I saw. I called my wife to come and stand next to me and see for herself. Right before her eyes she saw the walkway, the pool, a white wooden gazebo, a lagoon, a sandy beach and then the ocean. I knew without any doubt, this was the suite we were supposed to be in. I knew my dream was from God. God was up to something and I knew eventually I would know what it was. Everyone was amazed and my wife couldn't believe her eyes. "Honey", she said, "That's exactly what you told me you saw, but why did Jesus show you this?" I thought for a while and said to her, "To let me know we were supposed to be here." I continued to have dreams and open visions throughout our excursion.

On one of the following days we took an island tour. That particular morning we walked to the hotel lobby and waited for our team to come down. We found our car parked near the hotel front door and methodically climbed in finding any space to sit. It was a challenge to get seven people in a five seater car, but we did it, thank God for laps. I took the wheel and we proceeded to begin our island adventure. Everybody was extremely excited to see the island. While touring the island I saw an open market where I could see the most beautiful art pieces which I believed were painted by the indigenous people. I so wanted to stop and visit the marketplace but we had other sites to see and time was limited. I knew I would have to come back another day to explore. In the few hours touring the island we saw the most picturesque places the island had to offer. From turquoise waters with their white sandy beaches, beautiful green rolling mountains, to an old Castle which proudly stood against the ocean, like a fortress. We found the island to be enchanting.

We all needed to rest and have lunch so we decided to drive back to our hotel. While driving back I turned to my wife and shared with her God had given me an open vision. I told her, "I know our hotel has many restaurants and pools on the premises, but where I saw us eating lunch had a hedge of large skyrocket junipers which stood thirty feet high. On the back side of these junipers was a hotel with a large porte-cochere in front of its entrance and a restaurant which was right next to the hotel which had on display a-frame sign which read, "SOUP OF THE DAY". I tried to share every detail with her leaving nothing out.

We arrived at our hotel and freshened up for lunch. We asked the concierge if he could recommend a restaurant nearby. He recommended one on the premises which was walking distance. We were amazed they had so many restaurants to choose from. As we walked towards the recommended restaurant I noticed the view was exactly what I had seen in my open vision. I saw those skyrocket juniper trees, standing tall and proud. I couldn't wait to see what was behind them. Was my vision complete or was He telling me more? We walked behind the trees with such anticipation to see…YES!…the hotel with its porte-cochere and right next to the hotel the restaurant with an a-frame sign which read, "SOUP OF THE DAY". It was unbelievably amazing what God had shown me earlier and I was actually now standing in what He showed me. The Lord was allowing me to hear Him and He was having my spiritual eyes to be honed to see more clearly in the supernatural. I looked at my wife and team. They were astonished with what they were seeing and what I had revealed to them earlier…but unbeknownst to them, so was I. After lunch we sat at our table for a while and shared all the experiences we had during the tour. We returned to our suite and decided to rest for a while.

The next day I asked one of the pastors to ride with me in the little red car we had rented. My wife had asked me to be safe and not venture out. I sometimes become a bit adventurous, which has not at times been advantageous for me. I don't blame her for telling me this. She knows me quite well through past experiences! We arrived, parked the car and entered the marketplace. I was so excited to learn about the people and their customs. We could hear people bartering to receive the best deals for fresh fish, painted pottery and even strands of pearls of many colors. It was truly a wonderful experience to mingle with the local people of the island. The day was incredibly hot so I dressed in white shorts and a tangerine Hawaiian shirt. The vendors at the marketplace commented on my clothing and how they thought I must be an actor from America. Of course, I would tell them, "No, I'm not an actor, but thank you anyway." I kind of liked the attention they were giving me. With so many people giving me so many compliments, being true or not, my head began to swell with haughtiness. I caught myself walking around looking at my shirt and saying to myself, "My shirt is nice, and so are my shorts. I do look rather nice in them." Little did I know God was going to have to cut me down to size. God tells us in Proverbs 16:18, *"Pride goes before destruction, and a haughty spirit before a fall."*

As I was walking around the marketplace welcoming the compliments I seemed to expect, I felt something crawling on my back. I tried to brush it off with my hand hoping whatever it was would fall off. I realized it was inside my shirt and was actually crawling on my back. I began to jump around and scream like a little girl! I ripped off my shirt, threw it on the ground and stomped on it. Whatever it was I hoped it was dead. I realized it was still on my back and I yelled, "Help me, help me please!" I contorted and bent my body until this little boy slapped that large flying bug off of me. I ended up with a dirty Hawaiian shirt and found myself naked from my waist up in front of the whole marketplace! Many of the vendors and locals were laughing and telling me, "That bug doesn't bite, children play with them." I picked up my shirt, put it on and walked back to the car, of course with my head hanging down with embarrassment. God knows how to get your attention to help you stay humble. Thank you, Lord. Returning to the car I closed my eyes and asked God to forgive me for my pomposity.

You would think I would learn from this ordeal, but no! My wife did tell me not to be adventurous but across the highway I saw a small housing community and wanted to experience their culture. I wanted to mingle with them and learn more about them. I told my friend, "Hey, let's check out the community across the way, it looks interesting." He told me, "Your driving have at it!" So there we were driving across the two-lane highway into a dirt road headed to the entrance. I noticed all the homes looked similar. They looked as though they were made of adobe with curtains covering their windows and front doors. We drove awhile and lost our way. I was drawn to an old women sweeping the ground in front of her home and stopped to ask her for directions. I told her we were lost and if she would direct me to the entrance and/or exit of her community. She looked in the car and pointed to her ring finger and wrist and said, "You don't wear jewelry in this place. They will cut your finger or hand to get at those!" I said, "Thank you so much, you are so kind." She gave us the directions to exit her community. She said, "Make a right, go two blocks and make another right and at the end of the road make a left, remember make a left."

I waved bye to her and proceeded to follow her directions. I made a right and then another right and stopped at the end of the road to make a left but I heard the Lord tell me "NO" make a right. As I turned the corner making my right turn I saw an army stake truck come close behind me and another truck pulled in front of me. They tried to hold me captive because I wasn't able to go forward or even backwards. Men were coming out of the stake truck and I had only seconds to decide what to do. I turned the steering wheel all the way to my right and stomped on the gas pedal to the floorboard. As the men began to run towards us I managed to move out of their make-shift barricade and sped to the exit of the community. I thank God for His protection and words of direction. You see that old women had set me up. It was a trap! She told me to make a left but instead I heard the Lord tell me to turn right. She orchestrated those men to come after us, but I knew a God. I realized the community only had one way in and the same way out. If I had made a left it would have eventually placed me at a dead end. That was the trap the women planned for our demise. I thank the Lord for protecting us. I was so happy to be on the road going back to the hotel. I told my friend not to share this adventure with anyone especially my wife. I knew I would be in trouble so I elected to tell her later.

The following day we were scheduled to fly a 747 jet to Caracas, Venezuela and to board a nineteen seater propeller plane to visit Canaima National Park where the country boarders Brazil and Guyana. We all decided to go to bed earlier than usual to be able to wake up early and meet our 6:00 am flight. Around three in the morning, as all the others were fast asleep, I began to have yet another dream. I found myself standing in a dark room. Suddenly my wife staggered in the room wearing a green and white summer dress. She seemed to be quite pale and struggled to breathe. I asked her if she was okay, but she would just look at me with fear in her eyes. She seemed to be trying to tell me she was dying, so I pulled her into my arms and began to pray. I held her so tight I could feel her heartbeat pounding against my chest. She lovingly laid her head against my shoulder and wouldn't move away from my embrace. I prayed with all that I was worth asking God to heal my wife. I continued to pray in my heavenly language until I felt the release from God to stop. Loretta lifted her head from my shoulder and smiled. She said, "Honey, I'm fine. Don't worry." I kissed her and held her in my arms while thanking God for healing her.

God's large hand appeared in the room and held me, picking me up through the ceiling and placing me on the corner of Lemoran Avenue in the city of Pico Rivera, California, the street I lived on. I was standing at the corner and looked up and said, "Lord, I can't be here right now....I'm asleep in my hotel room in Isla de Margarita." He said with His powerful but yet gentle voice, "Go to your house, but pay close attention my son.....look and listen." Walking towards my house I recognized many of the homes I was passing. When I got closer to my house I stopped no more than thirty feet away and couldn't believe what I was seeing. My newly landscaped yard was completely ruined. My front yard had dirt piles and broken planters. I kept on thinking to myself, "Who could have done this?" The back yard, the front yard and even the side yards were in a state of upheaval. I was so upset because I had labored much to fix this yard. As I continued to walk around my house I noticed there were metal pieces lodged in the ground. Some were large while others were small. I couldn't determine where they came from until I pulled a portion out from the mound of dirt. It was a part of a planes wing. Gouged deep in my front yard was a gnarled piece of metal connected to the plane's engine which was still sparking. I realized a plane had crashed in my yard. As I stood there with my new found understanding I was overwhelmed as to what God had dropped into my spirit. I said to the Lord, "Oh no, I am going to suffer a plane crash, right? This is what you are trying to tell me?". The Lord said, "Yes my son, and speak no words to anyone."

I woke up completely wet with perspiration attributed to fear. "Please Lord...don't let me die. I don't want to die! Please not now." I reminded Him of when I was eight. You had me prophesy and proclaim that I had purpose and no one or anything would stop me or harm me. Even my commission You gave me at fourteen years of age, telling me You had elected me to go throughout the world, and through me You were going to heal a multitude of people. You also told me I would be like a Doctor but I wouldn't go to school for it. Oh Lord, You told me You would place power upon my hands. I can't die now. Jesus was silent. He wouldn't say a thing. I said, "Remember at thirty-three years old, I had a two and a half-hour visitation with You? You told me You were now going to separate me, sanctify me and consecrate me to have the authority to walk under Your Glory. You told me my ministry would be one of the largest and richest. No Lord, my time is not over." He continued in His silence.

I got on my knees and prayed and cried out for about an hour until I moved to my survival mode. "Wait!" I said, "I have many other flights to go on, maybe it's not this one. Yes, that's it, not this one." At around five o'clock in the morning my wife woke up and asked me if I was okay. I said, "Yes, I'm okay. Why do you ask?" She said, "You look like you have been crying. Are you feeling alright?" I told her it could be that I had been praying and communing with God. If she only knew what I was praying about, but God had made it clear to me I could not tell anyone.

She got up and began to make ready for our flight. She told me she would shower first and dress and then it would be my turn. While she was showering, I began to feel better and began to get excited to have the opportunity to see the monkeys, macaws and the tallest waterfall in the world, Angel Falls. I allowed myself to believe it was not this flight and I challenged myself then to make this day the best day of my life. When she came out of the dressing room wearing a green and white summer dress...it was the same one I saw in my dream. I knew then this was the flight which would crash. She asked me if I liked her dress because I was staring at it. "Oh, I was? Ah, yes, of course I like it. It's quite pretty, "She didn't know her dress was my sign that this plane was in fact our coffin.

I entered the bathroom, closed the door and fell to my knees and wept. I continued to pray asking, "God, where are You? I don't hear You, Lord." I pleaded with the Lord but He wouldn't reply. I got dressed and came out to be greeted by our group. We walked out of our suite to the airport shuttle which was parked in front of the hotel. One of my associate pastors commented he forgot to bring film other than the one which was in his camera. I looked at him and wanted to tell him not to worry because he wasn't going to be able to see them anyway. But I didn't, I couldn't because the Lord said not to tell anyone. So I told him we could probably find some at the airport. I would look at my wife as I sat next to her in the shuttle and desperately wanting to tell her how much I loved her, and how thankful I was for her giving me three beautiful boys.

We arrived at the airport and boarded our plane for Caracas and sat in our designated seats. My wife and I were seated towards the middle of the plane while the others were further to the back. I had forced a smile on my face to not alarm or give away our dreaded fate, but in the midst of this ordeal, deep inside of me, I was praying a mile a minute. The plane took off and began to climb to an elevation of ten-thousand feet. The flight attendant was offering drinks and snacks while pushing her cart. I began to hear a high-pitched beeping sound which lasted for about fifteen seconds and began to beep again. The flight attendant was nearing my row of seats when the plane shuttered and it shook the way a fish swims. It was not turbulence; this was something different. Again, the plane began to shutter but much stronger and longer. The seatbelt sign illuminated alerting us to secure our seat and seatbelt. I looked up at the head flight attendant in front of me who was trying to quickly strap herself in her seat. But right before she sat she took her right hand and waved at the flight attendant next to me, directing her to quickly find her seat. She took her hand and moved it across her neck and then pointed down signifying the plane was going down. The flight attendant seeing this shoved the cart forward having all the refreshments fall to the ground.

My wife asked, "What's going on?" I said, "Don't worry Sweetheart, just pray. Everything is going to be fine." She grabbed my arm and stayed close. The lights in the plane began to flicker and eventually they went out. The air stopped, making it difficult to breathe and even worse, I realized the engines of the plane had stopped also. The plane began to lose its thrust and fall straight down. What I found quite odd was everyone else other than my wife and team seem to be unaware of what was happening. I couldn't understand why all the passengers did not react or display any emotion. What was wrong with them? They seemed to be in a comatose state of mind. My wife even asked the man sitting next to her when the plane shuttered if he thought it was unusual. He turned to her and said, "Yes, it was unusual." He never showed fear or great concern."

As the plane continued to fall, I prayed out loud calling on the Lord to help us! It seemed as though we were doomed to die. I yelled out, "No God, You did not tell me this to die but to live! I command angels to hold up this plane." Instantly, the plane stopped and was suspended in midair. I know this sounds insane, but that is exactly what happened. My wife looked out of the window and said, "We are not moving, we're standing still!" This ordeal lasted for twenty minutes. It seemed like an eternity. I said to the Lord, "You told me you wouldn't give me anything I couldn't handle, and I believe I've reached my limit!" I prayed, "Lord, let this plane start and land safely at Caracas Airport." Instantly, the engines started, which I know it is aerodynamically impossible, but they were on. The plane began to climb again to a safe altitude and in a few minutes we were safely landing. Everyone grabbed their carry-on and disembarked, except for me. I needed to see what had happened.

As I waited for the pilot to come out of the cockpit, two soldiers came in and found the pilot unconscious in his seat. They dragged the pilot out by his arms and into an awaiting ambulance. I couldn't blame the pilot, he was trying to fly a plane that wouldn't fly. As the soldiers were passing me I questioned them on what happened to the pilot. They told me to get off the plane. I followed them off the plane to the information desk and inquired about our flight. They told me they didn't know what happened but twenty minutes could not be accounted for. How could I possibly tell them we were being held suspended in the air and I prayed for angels to hold up our plane. How could I tell them God gave me a dream last night about this horrific calamity.

Upon rejoining my group, my wife asked me, "What happened to you? Where were you? What took you so long?" I replied, "I stayed back on the plane to see if the pilot could tell me something about our flight but he was carried out unconscious by two soldiers and I followed them out. I went to the information desk and inquired of our plight, and they only informed me that twenty minutes were unaccounted for in the flight log. She said, "I am not going to get on a plane again," to which I replied, "You have to. We eventually have to fly back home." I told her, "God told me we were going to have a plane crash but not to tell you or anyone." She said, "I will only get on a plane again if you promise to tell me if God would ask that of you again!" I quickly promised, "Yes, absolutely." But knowing if He would ask that of me again, I would submit, be obedient, and speak no words. Forgive me Lord for lying but It was the only way I would be able to convince her to board another plane.

I mentioned to my wife I needed a few moments alone with God. I found a private place where I felt comfortable enough to be able to cry out to God. There was so much I needed to ask Him. Why did I go through this? Finally, I began to hear His still small voice. He began to speak. After all this time praying and crying out to Him to hear Him, He said to me, "My son you have fared well. I tested you, my son. I tested you the way I have tested many men of old. It is those I have elected, separated, sanctified, and consecrated to have the authority to walk under My Glory. You my son are one of them. I had to see if you would be obedient, and you were." He said to me, "You never thought nor considered not even once, to not board the plane. For the way, level and dimension in which I am going to use you, I had to see if I could trust you. I will move through you in a great and powerful way, my son. I had to allow this test to see if you were completely trustworthy. I wanted to see if you would offer your life to Me, and you chose to get on that plane. Just like my son Abraham who offered his son Isaac. He trusted Me and in the same way you proved to Me, that I can trust you." After hearing the Lord explain it that way, although my heart was still unsettled I was thankful I had passed the test. I told the Lord, "Whatever you need to do to me to allow me to walk with you and serve you. It is well with my soul."

When I got back to my wife and the team, there was something they wanted to tell me. They said looking out the window in the back of the plane they saw three large angels holding up the plane on their backs. One on each wing and one under the center of the plane. Wow! That was my prayer, which they didn't know! Our mighty God is so good. I told them God orchestrated this plane ordeal. I told them God was testing my obedience and I passed the test. He said He trusts me! Can you believe that? He trusts me. My associates were asking me, "But why didn't you tell us?" I said, "No, that was part of the test! He told me not to tell anyone. Do you all forgive me?" They all smiled and said, "We have to."

We waited for our next plane. It was a nineteen seat propeller plane. It was such a beautiful plane. It was a type of airplane which was one I personally never had seen before. It was made of a shiny aluminum. I personally didn't like flying in small planes. You feel too much turbulence as it soars into the sky. We were headed to Canaima. The pilot flew at a low altitude so we could see the great rivers in the Amazonian region. During our flight I asked the Lord for a favor. I asked Him if He would give me a picture of Him. I know, you might be thinking again, that I am crazy, but many archeologist and hikers have taken pictures of the landscape and they have seen the face of Jesus which was made up of snow, rocks or trees. So, I asked the Lord to give me mine. As we came close to Angel Falls I began taking pictures of it and felt the small window near me wasn't allowing me to take great pictures. I slowly walked up to the cockpit and asked the pilot if I could take a picture from his vantage point. His side windows were much bigger and opened. I must tell you I, at that time, feared heights and for me to walk in that small plane towards the cockpit and wanting to take pictures through the open side window was ridiculously absurd. But he said, "Yes, of course you may". Without any fear or apprehension I took many pictures of the landscape, rivers and of Angel Falls.

After returning from our recent trip we invited friends and family to our home for dinner. It has been our tradition to do that to display the photographs from our travels. While talking to some of our guests, a precious woman of God waved me over pointing towards a few pictures I had taken and **asked**, "Did you take this?" I said, "Yes! Isn't Angel Falls beautiful?" She said, "Yes, but I'm not looking at the falls on the picture. Don't you see next to the falls is the face of Jesus?" I held the picture and saw the Lord's face and realized He had granted my request. His photograph, His face could be seen in the picture of **Angel Falls**. Wow! God Is Good. I was overwhelmed and wept. "Oh, But I Know a God."

Years later I was talking with a gentleman who was a member of our church about our travels. When I shared with him the story about the plane that wouldn't fly, he marveled over the fact that a plane was suspended for twenty minutes. He would ask me many times to tell him the story of the plane again. He told me he was speaking to a friend who was a commercial pilot and they were discussing many things about their life experiences. His friend, in the midst of their conversation, began to tell him once he was piloting a plane and saw a 747 jet beneath him to his left, not flying, but suspended in midair. He said it stayed in place and as he continued moving **passed**, it continued to stand still behind his line of vision. He said it was the strangest thing he had ever experienced flying. My friend, remembering my story asked the pilot, "Where were you when you saw that plane?" He said between Isla de Margarita and the north shore of Venezuela. My friend told him, "My pastor was in that plane. He said it stood still for twenty minutes." The pilot told him,

"Well, then I am a witness to it because I saw it. He speaks truth".

God began to show me through dreams and visions from the beginning of this trip, to test my obedience in helping me to trust the gifts He gave me. In 1 Peter 1:7 the Bible reads, *"These trials will show that your faith is genuine. It is being tested as fire tests and purifies gold."* Also, in Jeremiah 17:7 it teaches us, *"Blessed are those who trust in the Lord and have made the Lord their hope and confidence."* God wanted to see if I would be obedient even unto death. He didn't want me to die, He wanted me to live, but He was looking to see and calibrate my trust towards Him. Could my faith in Him go past my comfort, my understanding, my situation? I never thought of not getting on that plane. I leaned on not only what I knew but who I knew. I know God is omnipotent, omnipresent, and omniscient. Sometimes we must investigate to receive knowledge which helps our journey. These three words define what God is:

Omnipotent - God is all powerful.
In the book of Revelation 19:6 we read,

"Alleluia! For the Lord God Omnipotent reigns!"

The Greek word translated as "Omnipotent" is Pantokrator meaning all-ruling, the Almighty, and all powerful. In other words, God has unlimited power and the ability to do anything. He is supreme and preeminent. Scripture tell us of God's authority. We must agree He has all authority to do all His pleasure and to see the fulfillment of His plans without fail. (Isaiah 46:10-11). Many people say God cannot do all things. For discussion sake, *"God cannot lie"* as stated in Titus 1:2, and *"He cannot deny Himself"* 2 Timothy 2:13. He cannot act contrary to His nature, and I say, "Amen to that!"

Omnipresent - God is in all places.

Omnipresent means being present everywhere at the same time. Can this term be applied to God? What does Scripture tell us?

Or where can I flee from Your presence? If I ascend into heaven, You are there; if I make my bed in hell [the grave], behold, You are there. If I take the wings of the morning, and dwell in the uttermost parts of the sea, even there Your hand shall lead me, and Your right hand shall hold me" (Psalm 139:7–10). David answers the question beautifully: it is futile to search for a place to hide from the presence of God (and it is unwise to try—just ask Jonah!). In this sense, God's infallible word shows He is omnipresent—within His vast creation, there is no place where you can hide from His presence.

Omniscient - God is all knowing.

Omniscience is defined as "the state of having total knowledge, the quality of knowing everything." For God to be sovereign over His creation of all things, whether visible or invisible, He has to be all-knowing. His omniscience is not restricted to any one person in the Godhead—Father, Son, and Holy Spirit are all by nature omniscient.

God knows everything (1 John 3:20). He knows not only the minutest details of our lives but those of everything around us, for He mentions even knowing when a sparrow falls or when we lose a single hair (Matthew 10:29-30). Not only does God know everything that will occur until the end of history itself (Isaiah 46:9-10), but He also knows our very thoughts, even before we speak forth (Psalm 139:4). He knows our hearts from afar; He even saw us in the womb (Psalm 139:1-3, 15-16). Solomon expresses this truth perfectly when he says, "For You, You only, know the hearts of all the children of mankind" (1 Kings 8:39).

I have gone through many tests and trials in my life. Many were not welcomed but through them I gained much Godly wisdom and spiritual understanding from them. God predestines good works to come through us, so we have to be tested, honed, and made ready to handle the greater work ahead. God tested my faith in Him through my obedience to get on a plane which was to crash. He tested my ears to hear Him when I was barricaded by thieves. But, the dreams and visions were my prerequisites to prove to Him and to myself I could hear Him.

So when you are going through various trials count them all as joy. God is teaching, melting, and molding you for great work. (James 1:2-4) Faith pleases God, and when you please God, get ready for your great breakthroughs. I thank the Lord for what He has done and for what He is going to do in my life and in yours. I am forever thankful! "Because…'I know a God!'

CHAPTER 2

AN EAR TO HEAR

I have realized through my life's journey my life is not my own. This is what God confirmed to me in 1 Corinthians 6:19-20 *"Or do you not know that your body is the temple of the Holy Spirit who is in you, whom you have from God, and you are not your own? For you were bought with a price; Therefore glorify God in your body and in your spirit, which are God's."* I had never completely understood the different ways God would teach me there were many dimensions of Him. I slowly learned to trust Him and to welcome every opportunity in being in His Theophany (the visible and tangible presence of the Lord). My faith grew with every supernatural encounter He allowed me to have. It was what He wanted for me, to have great faith in Him.

I can remember, playing tetherball with my school buddies when I was eight years old. When the bell rang informing us our time of play was over, we knew we had to return to our classroom from recess. I saw all my friends hurriedly placing the handballs and soccer balls in the equipment bins and running to their classrooms, not to be late. I too, began to try to run towards my classroom when I found myself unable to move! It was as if my feet were stuck to the blacktop of our playground. The playground had emptied and I found myself alone, struggling to free my feet from the blacktop, but I just couldn't. I was afraid I was going to receive a tardy slip for being late.

I felt something inside of me. It seemed to give me an unction, as if it were being freed from the deepest part of my soul. I opened my mouth and these words came out with a strength, a boldness, and with authority. I said, "I was born with purpose, and not anyone, or anything will stop me, or harm me." After speaking out loud I remember thinking that was weird! I didn't know why I said that because it wasn't something I understood. The moment I finished prophesying and declaring my fate, my feet became unstuck. I was able to use my feet again. I began to run fast to my classroom and found my seat. The minute I sat down the tardy bell rang. I made it just in time!

I thought what happened to me was dumb and weird. As an eight-year-old boy, I didn't think it was God who had me speak those words. I decided not to share with anyone what I had just experienced because I myself couldn't explain it. God will find the right time and season in your life to speak to you. He will guide your steps for the activating and releasing of His call and His purpose in you, as He did to me at Murchison Street School playground. Throughout the Bible we read of many men and women God spoke to in activating and releasing His purpose and will in their lives. It reminds me of the scripture in Luke 4:18 "*The Spirit of the Lord is on me, because He has anointed me to proclaim good news to the poor. He has sent me to proclaim freedom for the prisoners and recovery of sight for the blind, to set the oppressed free.*" That is exactly what God had me do, proclaim my tomorrow.

In my formidable years my family and I lived in Boston Heights, which is a suburb of East Los Angeles. At that time, it was a family-oriented neighborhood. I can remember all the fun I had with my sister Diane. She was only one day short of eleven months older than I and my brother Steve seven years my junior. We and all of our neighborhood friends would play outside even after dark, games like hide-and-go-seek, kick-the-can, jump rope, and hop-scotch. My parents, Domingo and Elena, would either be looking at television peeking through the wooden framed screen door keeping their eyes on us or sitting on the front porch talking to the neighbors.

My parents raised us to have respect for ourselves as well as for others. We were taught to honor the elderly and help them if able. My Dad was known for being a hard worker, always providing well for his family, while Mother raised us to be able to take care of ourselves if need be, so we all were given chores after school. Mom was known for her impeccable home and bright white laundry hanging on the clothesline. She was extremely organized and gave us our after school chores. We were not always happy in doing them, but we knew if we didn't, retribution would quickly come.

I remember it was my week to dust and vacuum. I used Mom's old heavy Electrolux vacuum which in itself was hard work, pulling and tugging this monster of a machine, for even a fourteen-year-old boy. I can still hear the sound of the Electrolux giving off its contorted sounds which sounded to me like the cry of a wounded moose. Through these horrid sounds I still heard that familiar still small voice near my right ear. The voice I heard said to me, "Son, I have elected you to go throughout the world. Through you I will heal my people. You will be like a doctor but you will not go to school for it. My healing power shall I place upon your hands." I said to the Lord, "Yes Father!" I don't know why, but I knew the voice I heard was the Lord's voice. I wasn't afraid, because I heard that voice before.

I turned off the vacuum cleaner and turned to my mother who was seated at the dining table having her morning coffee. I said to her "Mom, you know what? I am going to be a Doctor when I grow up." She then commented it would be a wonderful profession for me to be in, since you were such a sickly child and were given a miracle which healed you through Dr. Oral Roberts. I replied "You're right. That's true, but I want to travel the world and see so many people healed." "Yes, son that would be great." I said, "And you know what Mom? I am not even going to go to school for it!" She immediately put her coffee cup down and stared at me and said, "Get back to work, you don't know what you're talking about....being a Doctor without going to school, healing people!" I know she thought I was crazy. I knew it! That's why at eight years old I didn't tell my friends what happened to me in the playground. Just like my mother, they would think I was crazy.

God confirmed my thinking of how people would think I was crazy in 1 Corinthians 2:14 *"But the natural man receiveth not the things of the Spirit of God for they are foolishness unto him: neither can he know them, because they are spiritually discerned."* It might have seemed I was going crazy or at the least quite foolish but I was commissioned by God that day. He gave me my assignment, my orders, my future.

The Bible tells us God has had people speak of things they didn't know or even knowledge they didn't have. This reminds me of Simon Peter in Matthew 16:15-17 where the Lord said to him *"But who do you say that I am? Simon Peter answered "*You are the Christ, the son of the living God." And Jesus said to him, "Blessed are you, Simon Barjona, because flesh and blood did not reveal this to you, but my Father who is in heaven. "

I believe the Lord gave me those words to prophesy out to the winds. I believe the year I brought forth the proclamation was a strategic age. God's words I spoke was the beginning of my ministry, my office, and His purpose in me. Why was God having me speak this out at eight years old? The number eight, in the Lord, means new beginnings. He had me speak that I was now in my season of new beginning or the beginning. Of course I didn't have a clue of what I did, but through the years the Lord has revealed this fact to me. I didn't know the Lord was teaching me how to hear Him so that I would be able to prophesy, and also give words of knowledge accurately, but always in His name.

Even though my ear began to hear the still small voice of the Lord my mind and flesh were still tied to the world. Before my grandmother Eloise passed away she would ask me to sing for the Lord. She had a beautiful relationship with her

God. She would tell me stories of Jesus and try to introduce me to Him and even though the stories were interesting, she couldn't remove me from believing in my dream. I wanted to be a professional singer or maybe even an actor. I thought my voice was for the world and I had a bright future in pursing just that. From fifteen years of age until thirty-three, I had gone to college, continued singing and acted in many city wide plays. I tried out for a Broadway show and was offered a leading role, but something was always missing.

I found the love of my life Loretta and that strengthened my life and gave me stability. I married, Loretta when she was eighteen and I twenty. We were young, in love and we had our whole lives ahead of us. God blessed us with our three sons. But something continued to plague me. A few years later my Grandmother became ill. She suffered a massive heart attack. I was devastated. I didn't want to lose her. I didn't know what I was going to do without her. She was my liaison to God. She knew her God and I thought I knew Him through her. I can remember the few days before her passing that all of the family were trying to comfort her. My mom, my grandmother's only daughter was at her bedside, with all the immediate family surrounding her. They asked me to come in and see what my grandmother wanted. She was in pain and in discomfort because of the tubes that were placed down her throat. I could hear from outside her room her crying and moaning because of the pain. None were able to understand her so they asked me to see if I could help because I was so close to her. It was so hard for me to walk in her room, but I did. As I approached her bedside she looked at me and I heard her say she needed two pillows because she couldn't breathe. I relayed the message to all to what she told me and they asked me, "When did mom say that?" I said, "Just right now". They all said, "No she didn't, we heard nothing but her moaning." I was hearing my grandmother and didn't know God had given me an ear to hear. Can you imagine God had opened my ears to hear her by the Spirit? I learned not only does the Lord speak to you audibly but he also allows you to be able to hear the thoughts of others when He finds it necessary.

Days later, Grandma's health seemed to be failing, weakening by the hour. I knew I had to see her again so we drove to the hospital and entered her room. She was sedated and was kept as comfortable as was medically possible. She looked at me and tried to convey something to me. It was hard this time to understand her but I was able to decipher some of her words. She said to me, "Will you sing for the Lord?" How could I tell my dying grandmother no. "Yes, Grandma I will!" She just stared at me and said, "I am not leaving this earth until you mean it and sing right now in front of me!" Wow! She knew how to have me sing to her God. So I took a song I knew, one which was not a hymnal or worship song and changed some of the words, and sang to her.

Tears began to fall from her eyes and she smiled at me. She was content because her grandson was finally to sing to the Lord. I kissed and hugged her knowing my hug and kiss would probably be the last ones I would be able to give her. Not many days after my grandmother passed and I was in a deep mourning. My grieving was deep, my heart broken, and peace could not be found in me.

I was thirty-three years old happily married, with three beautiful sons. I had a good paying job, a beautiful home and a new car. Everything on the surface seemed to be perfect. From the outside many would see my life as successful but from the inside I was dying. I began to go into a deep depression which held hands with panic attacks and anxiety. I went to Doctors, Psychiatrists, Sociologists and took all the medications they prescribed. None of it seemed to sedate the emptiness and despair which continued to gnaw into my innermost being.

I would sit at night in front of the television just to escape, never remembering what I saw. I was viewing television and began to surf the channels trying to find something interesting to watch. When I would find a movie the channel would switch by itself. It would move to channel 40, TBN Christian Television. I thought, "That's strange my controller must have been stuck." I changed the channel back to what I was watching. I watched my program for less than a minute and it changed channels again by itself, back to TBN. But, this time, I heard a tele-evangelist speaking and saying there is a young man who is sitting in his den in the dark watching and hearing him right now. I thought, "There's a lot of young men, a lot of dens, and a lot of dark rooms. I'm not falling for that! Not me, I wasn't born yesterday." He said "It is your time to come to know your Lord and Savior. You are going to feel His presence fall all over you." A second after he said that, I felt this warm and tingly feeling run down from my head all the way to my feet. I didn't understand it, but I knew it was God's presence. I fell to my knees in my darkened den and prayed the sinner's prayer, as he guided me. I was now born again, but that part of me still remained my secret.

My wife and I were not church goers unless there was a funeral, wedding, or special religious event. My religion, at the time, did not believe in tongues or laying on of hands. It was not in any way a charismatic church. So, I kept my new found conversion a secret. I was happy and knew something had changed in my life.

The following morning I woke up and decided to mow my lawn. I was out there mowing, and noticed an old red truck coming down my street and it parked in front of my house. I recognized the man who was stepping out of his truck. It was the manager of the warehouse where I was employed. He put his hand out to greet me and said "Hi Al, how are you?" I looked at him and said, "Oh, I'm fine, how are you?" After shaking hands, I asked him how he knew where I lived? He said "You might think what I am going to tell you is kind of strange but this is what happened. I was driving from work to get home but my truck wouldn't let me drive." I said, "What, your truck didn't let you drive?" I thought trucks didn't drive themselves. He said, "I would steer my truck to go straight but my steering wheel would start to turn right. It seemed to have a mind of its own. I would try to turn the wheel but it would not allow me to. I just prayed and asked the Lord to help me with this truck, when the truck turned by itself down your street and parked in front of your house. That's when I saw you mowing your lawn. That's my story Al and as God is my witness everything I am telling you is true. I know it sounds quite absurd but that is exactly what happened. Your right! I didn't even know where you lived. I don't know why I am here?" I said "I do." Maybe it's because last night something great happened to me. You see, I was looking at TBN and this tele-evangelist came on and he said it was my time to know the Lord Jesus. So, I invited the Lord into my heart to be my Lord and Savior.

I rejoice with you, Al, on your new found life. God is going to bless you and your family because of what you did, last night. I said, "Hey, please don't talk too loud my wife might be hearing us. She doesn't know about my born again experience, yet." He said, "Oh ok, well I have to go now, but congratulations. If you want to know more about the Bible come to one of my Bible classes on Wednesday at 7:00 pm." I said, "Okay maybe one of these days but with one condition....don't ask me any questions about the Bible because I don't know anything about it. I don't want to be embarrassed." "Oh, no Al, you don't have to worry, I won't do that to you, you have my word." In my mind, I really didn't intend to go to his Bible class. So saying I might, was just me being kind.

Three weeks passed and I decided to check out his Bible study. I told my wife I heard of a Bible study my friend from work was having in his house and I wanted to check it out and asked her if she wanted to go with me. She said "No thank you I'm not going to that, but you go if you think you need it". I kissed her goodbye and drove to the city of Montebello and looked for his house. I found the place and walked in and found a mature group of believers. They were all very nice and seemed so happy. They all welcomed me with hugs and thanked me for being there. I found a seat right in the middle of everyone to camouflage myself.

They began to sing a song which had the same words that were sung over and over again. I was not accustomed to churches which sang so loud and so enthusiastically, so it was a bit weird for me at first. They sang Hallelujah, Hallelujah, Hallelujah, Hallelujah, and again they repeated the word Hallelujah until they changed it to Lord I love you, Hallelujah, Lord I love you, Hallelujah. I do have to say it was easy to sing with them because it was the same words over and over again. I could see than I was such a novice when it came to praising God. I never thought God would one day draw me closer to Him because of song.

After the songs were finished, an elderly man in his late eighties raised his hand and asked the Pastor if he would be able to ask him a question. He said he was getting up in age, and would love to have the answer to this question he had for years. The Pastor asked him what the question was? He replied, "I want to know the method of operation and the correlation to the Triune God." I thought, wow, Triune huh....I didn't know God had another first name called Triune. That's how little I knew about the Bible and the Lord....not much! The Pastor asked if there was anyone who was able to answer that question. I took my red Bible which I found in my closet and with my left hand held the Bible close to my face. I began to act as if I was preoccupied in reading it. Then I heard the Pastor ask me "Brother Al, you know?" I was shocked and surprised he would ask me if I knew the answer, because he gave me his word...not to embarrass me. I took my face away from my Bible and saw my right arm had betrayed me. It was raised high in the air, signifying I knew the answer. I quickly brought down my arm. Pastor again asked me "Al you know the answer to the question?" I was just about to say no, when again, just like what happened to me at eight, and at fourteen, was now happening to me again, but now at thirty-three years of age. I felt an unction deep inside of me. I looked at the Pastor and said to him, "Yes I know the answer!" He said with a grin, "Why don't you stand and tell us all, since you seem know it."

I stood up with a boldness and authority which only God could have given me and answered the question. To think a young man only in the Lord for three weeks being able to answer such a difficult and complicated question. What could I really know about that? But what came out of my mouth was; "The method of operation and the correlation to the Triune God is likened to the perfect sentence in the English language. God is the perfect sentence. Jesus Christ is the noun the name, the Holy Spirit is the verb, the action, the power. You take one out and the sentence is incomplete. They all have their own method of operation just like the sentence, with its noun, and verb. If one is taken out it disqualifies the whole sentence. God is all, the perfect sentence, God the Father, God the Son, and God the Holy Spirit. The noun is the name Jesus Christ, the name above every name." Philippians 2:9-11 *"Wherefore God also hath highly exalted him, and given him a name which is above every name, that at the name of Jesus every knee should bow, of things in heaven, and things in earth, and things under the earth, and that every tongue should confess that Jesus Christ is Lord, to the Glory of God."* In the book of Micah 3:8" *But as for me, I am filled with power, with the Spirit of the Lord, and with justice and might, to declare to Jacob his transgression, to Israel his sin."* That is the method of operation and the correlation of the Triune God.

The Pastor asked me, "Who taught you that?" I replied "No one!" He said, "Did you read this in a book?" "No, it just dropped inside of me, I just knew." He said "God is truly going to use you, Al." I was equally surprised of the answer I gave, as were those who surrounded me, who also heard it. This is yet another example of how God gives us an ear to hear Him. This time it was not an audible voice heard by my ear. It was His voice that fell inside of me which I call today my knower.

I continued to attend his Bible class and a few months later I became a member of his church. I began to have a deep desire to know more of God and His Word and began to study the Word of God. The Bible tells us in 2 Timothy 2:15 *"Study to show thyself approved unto God, a workman that need not to be ashamed, rightly dividing the word of truth."* God allowed me to be the recipient of His knowledge which is why the answer was so simple to a complicated question. The simplicity only proved how profound the answer was, and that's when I began to recognize I was beginning to know my God and to have an ear to hear Him.

God, throughout my life, has encouraged my ear to hear Him through my experiences and encounters with Him. In the Bible Samuel heard the voice of God, but did not recognize it until he was instructed by Eli (1 Samuel 3:1-10). Even Gideon had a physical revelation from God, and he still doubted what he had heard to the point of asking for a sign, not once, but three times (Judges 6:17-22, 36-40). Many tell us to hear God's voice we must belong to God. Jesus said, *"My sheep listen to my voice; I know them, and they follow me"* (John 10:27). Many say it is those who belong to Him - those who have been saved, born-again by His grace through faith in the Lord Jesus. I was eight years old and wasn't born again, I wasn't saved, but I heard His still small voice. Samuel according to Josephus the Jewish historian, at twelve heard God calling him Samuel, Samuel.

The Lord tells me before I was formed in my mother's womb, God knew me (Jeremiah 1:5). *"He created my innermost being, he knit me together in my mother's womb."* (Psalm 139:13) *"From my birth, while I was still in the womb, I cast myself into God's loving hands. He has been my God since I was in my mother's womb. I will ever praise Him, my God and Heavenly Father."* (Psalm 71:6). *"We are God's workmanship, created in Christ Jesus to do good works, which God prepared in advance for me to do "*(Ephesians 2:10). *"This is why, I will shout this throughout the world, I will trust in the Lord with all my heart, I will lean not on my own understanding; in all my ways I will acknowledge you, Lord, knowing, since I was in my mother's womb, you have straightened the path for me."* (Proverbs 3:5-6)

When the Lord said in John 3:16 that He gave His only begotten son, because He loved the world, the world is you and me, that's everyone. God is not calling us into a religion but into a relationship, having Jesus Christ be our Lord and Savior. Whatever persuasion of religion you believe in, complement it, with Jesus Christ being your Lord and Savior. Let God change, rearrange, remove, or add and subtract, whatever is necessary for you to come closer to the true King of kings. I pray He gives you and ear to hear Him.

One night in my den, my friend, who was one of my back-up vocalists and I were talking and joking around having wonderful fellowship. We noticed all my floors were being covered by billowing white smoke which formed mini whirlwinds. It was so thick we were not able to see through them. These divine whirlwinds were about two feet high and completely covered my den, living room, and dining room. I thought at first my house was on fire. My floors were made of hardwood and I thought somehow they caught on fire from the crawlspace below.

We both seemed to be paralyzed with fear but still captivated with curiosity. We didn't know what to do, when I heard that familiar still small voice, yet again. I dropped to my knees and said to my friend, "Get on your knees, this is the Glory of God which we are seeing. This is His presence, and you don't know if this is the only time you will experience such a high dimension of His glory." My friend said, "Al, can you hear me?" I looked at him and said, "Yes, why would you ask me that, right now? We have Jesus Christ right here with us!" He said, "Al, you're not moving your lips when you talk, but I can hear you." I looked at his mouth, as he was talking to me, and he too, was not using his mouth to speak. I could hear him clearly, he could hear me, but no longer did we have the need to use our mouths. We didn't decide not to use our mouths, it just happened. The Bible tells us in Psalm 139:4 *"For there is not a word in my tongue, but, lo, O Lord, thou knowest it altogether."* Psalm 139:2 *"You know my sitting down and my rising up, you understand my thought afar off."*

In my encounter with the Lord, His presence was so saturated, so pure, and so holy, we were in a most heavenly realm. We were experiencing a higher dimension in Him, all around us seemed to stand still. 1 Corinthians 2:14-16 reads *"This is what we speak, not in words taught us by human wisdom but in words taught by the Spirit, explaining spiritual realities with Spirit taught words. The person without the Spirit does not accept the things that come from the Spirit of God but considers them foolishness, and cannot understand them because they are discerned only through the Spirit."* (1 Corinthians 2:13-14) We were so close to Jesus that all was being done in the Spirit.

I looked around the room observing all the whirlwinds. Each whirlwind moved in its own axis, but was in unison with all the others. The presence of the Lord was so pure, radiant, and holy, all I could do was bow at His feet, with my face towards the ground. His Holiness only magnified my impurity, my uncleanness. I felt as if I, in comparison to Him, was nothing more than a complete filthy, dirty rag. Isaiah 64:6 describes exactly how I felt bowing before the King of kings and the Lord of lords by saying *"But we are all as an unclean thing, and all our righteousness are as filthy rags, and we all do fade as a leaf, and our iniquities, like the wind, have taken us away."*

What seemed so different and peculiar in my home was the stillness which was seen. My coffee table was still, as if bowing, my sofa and chairs were still, as if they were bowing, my fireplace was still and seemed to be bowing to the King. I know you might think I must have lost all my marbles, but that is what we saw. It was as if the Lord placed us in a completely different realm, level, or dimension. The Bible tells us in

Philippians 2:10 *"That at the name of Jesus every knee should bow, of those who are in heaven, and on earth, and under the earth, and that every tongue should confess that Jesus Christ is Lord, to the glory of God the Father."* I could not comprehend how my house seemed to be standing still, when everything around me before didn't move.

The Lord told me everything in heaven, on earth, and under the earth He created. The Lord said to me all I have created was made by my matter, with atoms. I later studied to prove what the Lord had told me and found out atoms are the basic units of matter and the defining structure of elements. Atoms are made up of three particles: protons, neutrons and electrons. Virtually all the mass of the atom resides in the nucleus. The nucleus is held together by the "strong force", God's divine creative power. The atoms that make up all masses, like sofas, chairs, and fireplaces are continually moving, pushing, and vibrating. We, with our natural eye, can't see them move, but being lifted to a higher divine dimension, I could see everything stands still and bows before the King, when He is ushered in, but through the natural eye everything is still.

As we knelt down and raised our hands in this most divine ambience, I once again heard that familiar still small voice. The Lord spoke to me saying "I have waited for such a time as this my son. I am now going to SEPARATE YOU, SANCTIFY YOU, and CONSECRATE YOU, so you will have the AUTHORITY to walk under my Glory." I couldn't believe my ears. The Lord told me He is allowing me to walk under His Glory, Wow! He told me my ministry was going to be one of the biggest ministries in the world and one of the wealthiest. In me I thought, Really? I don't know how, but I will believe. He said "Your ministry will be likened to my son Oral Roberts but higher in my Spirit and deeper in my Glory. He said "I am going to give you the rough and the tough, my son." I said "Alright Lord but I was never a rough type teenager, so I don't know if they would identify with me." "No, my son not them, those who have nothing, they come to me easily. I am going to give you those who have everything but they don't have me. You will be with Presidents of Countries, and high dignitaries of different nations." There were so many things the Lord shared with me about our tomorrows. He said in due season these things shall be revealed. My encounter with the Lord lasted for two and a half hours.

As we sat on the sofa, we saw the whirlwind which was with us began to rise up and cover the ceiling. My friend told me, "Al, above your head a pipe is forming from the Glory cloud and it's coming down towards your head." At the moment it touched my head and came in me, it was as if a 440 bolt of electricity was going through me. It was so strong it made me double over and moan with pain. Every fifteen seconds I would have a bolt of His Glory flow through me, which continued for two hours. After the two hours of the Lord dousing me with His glory, He left and everything reverted back to our dimension, to our reality. I looked around the room in awe to what just had taken place. Then my front door began to shake and creek. The door began to pulsate and expand, as if it were made of rubber. I knew satan was on the other side of my door. I yelled out, " satan you can't touch me or hurt me, *for greater is He that is in me, than He that is in the world.*" (1 John 4:4) I fearlessly invited him to come in, but he wouldn't. He in a split of a nano second was in my back yard shaking my French doors and he began to scrape his fingernails on the window bringing forth this eerie sound, but I was not afraid of him and I said to him again, "*Greater is He that is in Me, than he that is in the world.*" My French doors shook even more and he went to another window and did the same. I finally said to him, "*Who can come against me, when God is before me?*" I was quoting Romans 8:31 "*What, then, shall we say unto these things? If God be for us, who can be against us?*" Satan departed instantly, because he knew I was not afraid of him.

The Lord Jesus Christ of Nazareth was ushered back in my home, with all His Glory and told me, "You have fared well my son, not even satan are you afraid of". When you have the Lord so close to you, when your relationship with Him is so intimate, you begin to possess a knowing, an assurance, a boldness, an authority, to know who God is in you, and who you are in God.

To hear the voice of the Lord is essential, paramount, and capitol in your life. We all need direction, we need instruction, we need divine communication. Throughout my journey I have seen God speaks to all of us, but how many really listen? Jesus placed much emphasis upon how we hear. Jesus said, *"He that hath ears to hear, let him hear."* (Matthew 11:15). In James 1:18 and 19 it reads, *"He chose to give us birth through the word of truth, that we might be a king of first fruits of all he created. My dear brothers and sisters, take note of this: Everyone should be quick to listen, slow to speak and slow to become angry".* I want to continue to be quick to listen and hear my Father. I don't want to miss my time, my chance, my opportunity to serve the Lord.

When I think of it, I prophesied my destiny at eight, received my commission at fourteen, and then was separated, sanctified, and consecrated at thirty-three years of age. Oh, I thank you Lord. I told the Lord, "Thank you for choosing me first" and He replied, "I didn't choose you first." "What? You didn't, well thank you for choosing me second." Again He said, "But I didn't, you were not second but third." I was a little taken aback and wanted to be God's first. Then the Lord said, "You were the only one of the three which heard me, stood up and said, "yes!" So, when you said yes, you became my first." Thank you Lord for giving me an ear to hear.

CHAPTER 3

FAITH TO RAISE THE DEAD

he Bible tells us Jesus performed many miracles, from the blind seeing, the deaf hearing, to even raising the dead. During Jesus Christ's earthly ministry, He touched and transformed countless lives. The four Gospels, Matthew, Mark, Luke, and John record thirty-seven miracles which He did. These accounts represent only a small number of the multitudes of people who were made whole by our Savior. The closing verse of the Book of John says, "*Jesus did many other things as well. If every one of them were written down, I suppose that even the whole world would not have room for the books that would be written.*" When Jesus turned water into wine at the wedding feast at Cana, He performed His first miracle, as the Apostle John records in the book of John. This miracle, showing Jesus' supernatural control over physical elements like water, revealed His Glory as the Son of God and marked the beginning of His public ministry. Here are the thirty-seven miracles Jesus performed. Some are spoken in more than one gospel, but I will give one of the books for reference.

1. Jesus Turns water to wine.   John 2:1-11
2. Jesus Heals an official's son.   John 4:43-54
3. Jesus Drives out an evil spirit.   Mark 1:21-27
4. Jesus Heals Peter's mother-in-law.   Matthew 8:14-15
5. Jesus Heals many sick at evening.   Matthew 8:16-17
6. First Miraculous Catch of fish.   Luke 5:1-11
7. Jesus Cleanses a man with leprosy.   Mark 1:40-45
8. Jesus Heals a Centurion's servant.   Luke 7:1-10
9. Jesus Heals a paralytic.   Matthew 9:1-8
10. Jesus Heals a man's withered hand.   Luke 6:6-11
11. Jesus Raises a widow's son in Nain.   Luke 7:11-17
12. Jesus Calms a storm.   Mark 4:35-41

13. Jesus Casts demons into a herd of pigs.   Matthew 8:28-33
14. Jesus Heals a woman in the crowd.   Luke 8:40-42
15. Jesus Raises Jairus' daughter to life.   Mark 5:21-24
16. Jesus Heals two blind men.   Matthew 9:27-31
17. Jesus Heals a man unable to speak.   Matthew 9:32-34
18. Jesus Heals an invalid at Bethesda.   John 5:1-15
19. Jesus Feeds 5,000   .   John 6:1-15
20. Jesus Walks on water.   John 6:16-21
21. Jesus Heals many sick in Gennesaret.   Mark 6:53-56
22. Jesus Heals a demon-possessed girl.   Matthew 15:21-28
23. Jesus Heals a deaf and dumb man.   Mark 7:31-37
24. Jesus Feeds 4,000.   Matthew 15:32-39
25. Jesus Heals a blind man at Bethsaida.   Mark 8:22-26
26. Jesus Heals a man born blind.   John 9:1-12
27. Jesus Heals a boy with a demon.   Luke 9:37-43
28. Miraculous Temple Tax in a fish's mouth.   Matthew 17:24-27
29. Jesus Heals a blind, mute demoniac.   Matthew 12:22-23
30. Jesus Heals a crippled woman.   Luke 13:10-17
31. Jesus Heals a man with dropsy/sabbath.   Luke 14:1-6
32. Jesus Cleanses ten lepers.   Luke 17:11-19
33. Jesus Raises Lazarus from the dead.   John 11:1-45
34. Jesus Restores sight to Bartimaeus.   Mark 10:46-52
35. Jesus Withers the fig tree.   Matthew 21:18-22
36. Jesus Heals a servant's severed Ear.   Luke 22:50-51
37. Second Miraculous Catch of fish.   John 21:4-11

These supernatural acts of love and power drew people to Jesus, revealing His divine nature. They opened up the hearts of many to the message of salvation and caused many to glorify God.

I have always wanted to see miracles before my eyes. I would cry out to God to allow me to be used as a vehicle, for Him to flow through me, His power, His healing, His miracles. I read in John 14:12-14 *"Truly, truly, I say to you, whoever believes in me will also do the works that I do; and greater works than these will he do, because I am going to the Father. Whatever you ask in my name, I will do it."* These words of Jesus, as perplexing as they are at one level, are powerfully inspiring and encouraging. Consider what He is telling you and me. Jesus tells us we can perform the same miracles and healing He did, and even greater ones than He did, in His name.

I took hold of His Word and truly believed what He told me. I began to pray for the sick, in Jesus name and they were being healed before my eyes. My faith continued to grow as I saw God move through me. I saw legs growing, cancerous tumors disappearing, AIDs vanishing from people. With my growing faith in the Lord I began to see Him defy science through me, as He continued to use me. From praying down rain with no clouds in the sky similar to Elijah, to seeing God have me speak to a hurricane to calm it down, immediately, which was likened to when Jesus calmed the storm. The more I saw, the more I wanted. I knew the scriptures were alive and all powerful. I knew if God told me to move a mountain, I knew that I would be able to. Luke 17:5-7 reads *"The Apostles said "Increase our faith". And the Lord said, "If you had faith like a mustard seed, you would say to this mulberry tree, "Be uprooted and be planted in the sea", and it would obey you."* and also in the book of Mark 11:23 *"Truly, I say to you, whoever says to this mountain, be taken up and thrown into the sea, and does not doubt in his heart, but believes that what he says will come to pass, it will be done for him."* I began to run with great faith in God's word. Every time I would see a miracle my faith would rise to higher heights, and when a child was healed of a disease through my hands and in the name of Jesus, I would marvel at how good and powerful our God was, is, and will always be.

I would love to share with you some remarkable stories of some of my experiences of miracles and healing. I pray these experiences I had will increase your faith as it has for me, to even raise the dead.

MAN IN THE VAN

I was driving around in the city with a long list of errands I had to do when I noticed my gas gauge was registering empty. I immediately looked for the closest gas station, because I didn't want to be left stranded. I began to pray and ask God to help me find a gas station soon, "Please don't let my car stall", because I knew the tank was very close to being empty. I tend to be a little picky on the type of gas I use in my car because sometimes the off-brands tend to have the car engine ping and have less power. As I continued to drive, probably on fumes, I saw an off-brand gas station and I said, "Hallelujah!" I didn't normally frequent this off-brand gas station but, I didn't have the luxury of choosing. It's either get this gas now and drive away or drive away and walk for gas later. I chose to get this off-brand gas now, I'm sure you too would have concurred.

As I parked under the gas station canopy near the pump, I noticed an old man in an old white van who had parked next to me, across the small island. I got out of my car and took out my money from my wallet to pay for my gas. In those days this particular station didn't have machines which would accept monies, just gas station attendants who would attend to your gas purchase. I know I'm dating myself, but gas stations before would even provide attendants who would pump gas for you, too. Remember, I was much younger then, too. As I gathered my monies and began to walk towards the attendant, the old man in the van yelled out to me and said, "Hey you, take these four dollars and tell the teller I am going to use gas pump number four." I looked at him, and at that moment, in my mind, I was thinking of telling him, "You take your own money to her, who do you think I am? I'm not your slave, you have legs, you take it to her, Mister!" But, God held my tongue. The Lord said, "Help this man". I said to the old man, "Absolutely Sir", and reached out and took his four dollars and walked towards the attendant to pay.

Upon returning from paying for our gas purchase, I saw the man was slowly getting out of his van. He held two crutches under his arms and in the process of reaching the ground he was moaning with pain. I began to pump my gas and noticed as he struggled to pump his gas, his right leg was deformed. Through his pants I could see his leg was swollen in some parts and skinny in other areas. I said, "Thank you Jesus for not allowing me to tell this old man what I was thinking, telling him he had legs to pay for his gas himself." I felt such a strong compassion for this old man.

I finished pumping my gas and asked the old man if he needed me to help him back in his van? He said, "I do, you can help me, give me a new leg." I asked him what was wrong with his leg. He said, "I have had problems with this leg for many years," as he pointed to his left leg. "I've gone through surgeries on this old leg but the surgeries haven't worked." With his blue eyes filling with tears, he said, "I just left my Doctor's office and he gave me some bad news." I wanted to hug him and comfort him, but, I didn't know if he would let me. I decided not to, and told him I was so sorry to hear that. He put his head down and told me the Doctor said the only thing left to do is to amputate his leg, way up to here, pointing towards the area below his hip. "Sir, have you thought of maybe going to someone to pray for you?" "Yes, I tried that, but it didn't work. I don't believe in that stuff anyway. I've already been to a priest and it didn't work." I asked him, "Please, would you allow me to pray for you? God gave me the gift of healing and miracles." I said, "If what I am telling you is true it can save your leg, but if I'm a charlatan then there's no harm and no foul. Please let me pray for you!" He climbed up into his van and looked at me and shook his head. I again said, "Okay what if I am right and telling you the truth! You could be letting your chance pass you by. You know this right now could be God." He responded, "Okay, pray". I opened the van door and placed my hands on his leg. I prayed, "Father I come before your throne, in the name of your son Jesus Christ of Nazareth. I lift up this man to you. You know him my Lord, you created him. I apply the blood of the lamb, the blood that still runs from Calvary to his leg. I pray for a creative miracle, my Lord. I pray this healing will heal his leg and also his heart. Let him know you are a God who loves him. I pray this in the name of Jesus."

I opened my eyes and the old man in the van began to cry. He was trying to tell me something but his sobs would not allow him to. He stepped out of the van and explained, "I don't have any more pain!, I can walk!, my leg has been made new!" I yelled out, "Thank you Jesus! He told me "You don't understand. All my joints, my toes, my ankle and knee were fused together. I can now move them!" He gave me a big bear hug and picked me up in the middle of the public gas station. He was twirling me around, the way a father would twirl his young son. This precious man thanked me with all his heart and left with a big smile, a new leg, and a renewed heart for God.

Every experience and encounter I have had with God has always been for instruction to develop more of God in me. The Bible tells us Jesus is our example of how we are to be. We are to take on the character of our Lord Jesus Christ. A Christ-like character is the ultimate goal of all Christians. If we settle for anything less, we miss our opportunity to any spiritual growth. I am reminded when Paul told Timothy the purpose of his teaching was to develop character in those he taught. Paul told Titus to do the same thing, "*Now you must tell them the sort of character which should spring from sound teaching*" (Titus 2:1). God always builds character in our lives by allowing us to experience situations where we are having to make a choice to either do right or wrong, good or bad. In any case our choices will either help us become mature or immature.

Apostle Paul tells us in Galatians 5:22-23, "*But the fruit of the Spirit is love, joy, peace, patience, kindness, goodness, faithfulness, gentleness and self-control*". The fruit of the Spirit is the perfect picture of Christ. He is all nine fruits. I know I have had to learn many times the hard way, how to react to situations or respond to adversities and diversities. Whenever we choose to respond to a situation in God's way instead of following our natural inclination, we develop character. This is why He allows all kinds of character-building circumstances like; conflict, disappointment, difficulty, delays, temptation, and times in the valley to be about us.

The Lord began to teach me His love through this man in the van. He taught me His patience, His kindness, His self-control while I was helping this crippled man. I thank the Lord for His continued teaching. Not only did the man receive His healing on his leg, but I received healing of my character and through that a greater faith in God's word.

FLAT AS A PANCAKE

This mid-morning proved to be the start of a beautiful day. The sky was blue with white puffy clouds while the sun shined bright beckoning us to start our day. We all got up, rather late, and had our breakfast meal for lunch. The boys were laughing and telling on each other while we laughed at how silly they were acting. After breakfast the boys asked to go outside and play with their neighborhood buddies. I knew I had some errands to run around the city so I told my wife I would be back in a few hours.

I was happy to be back home after completing my errands and sat in my favorite chair and watched television. Later, I barbecued some chicken for dinner while my wife was in the kitchen making her famous macaroni salad with olives and cheese. It's her grandmother's recipe which was passed down to her by her mother. After eating, we were stuffed and content. Around six o'clock while the sun was still out, my wife told me she was scheduled to attend our church's women's pageantry practice. As my wife was preparing to leave, the boys asked me if they could go outside and play with Mark and Jason, their best friends. I said, Yes you may, but wash your hands first and be careful." Well, it didn't take them but a minute to run down the hall to the bathroom and wash up. They ran out the front door with their hands still dripping wet, while calling out to their friends they were on their way. My wife was now ready to leave and stopped to kissed me goodbye and got in the car. She honked the horn and yelled out, "Honey I can't find Toby, I think he's under the car." I said, "Sweetheart don't worry, cats know how to get out of the way. Just start the engine and Toby will get scared and run out from under your car." She said to me, "Are you sure, because I don't want to run over him" "No, don't worry, cats always run out!"

As she backed out of the driveway, I went back inside the house and then I heard a very loud screech. I thought to myself, it better not be the cat because I am going to be in trouble. I ran towards the car and my wife was yelling, "What was that?" I told her to stop and I would check. Well, I knew I was in BIG trouble. The car's back tire was over the little kitten. Poor Toby! He was smashed and bleeding. I said, "Don't look back, just go forward." She knew something was wrong and she looked back and tried to see through the car's side mirror. I continued to tell my wife, "Sweetheart just go forward," but every time she would go forward the car would roll back on the kitten. She did try to maneuver the car to just go forward but to Toby's demise, the car continued to roll back over him, three times. Toby was under the tire and as flat as a pancake. His body and head were crushed and he looked like road kill. Boy was I in trouble! Of all the kittens in the world, her kitten was the only one who didn't move fast enough.

My two oldest boys, Al Jr. and Brandon, ages thirteen and ten, with their two friends Jason and Mark heard Loretta screaming for her kitten who was dead. My youngest son Ryan who was six years old came running out of the house and circled Toby with the other boys. My wife was crying, as well as all of the other boys when she said to me it was all my fault. I told you, she said, "You needed to find him and remove him from under the car." Well, she did tell me to do that, but, I thought the kitten would just run out, from the sound of the engine. I was not feeling very good about this situation and they made me feel like I was a cat murderer. I told my wife, "Everything is going to be alright." One of the boys pointed his finger towards the cat and said, "How can everything be okay, Daddy Toby's dead!." "I know son, but I can pray for God to raise him from the dead." Quickly I thought to myself, did I say that? You're going to bring Toby back to life? Yes, yes I am in Jesus name! So, there I was with my foot in my mouth.....toes and all. I said I was going to raise this kitten to life in the name of Jesus.

I stood over Toby believing God to raise him up. I placed my hand over him and prayed, "Father in the name of Jesus I come against the spirit of death off of Toby. I command in Jesus Christ name that life come back upon him. I apply the blood of Jesus on this kitten and believe he will not have a scar or even a broken bone. Instantly, before everyone, the cat began to move as if I had a tube in him blowing him up like a balloon. Toby was being filled with life and he stood up. My boys, as well as my wife, kept on saying, "Praise Jesus!" The kitten came back to life and started walking and meowing. At first Toby walked crooked and slowly but within a few hours the kitten was running and playing without any trace of injury. Jesus raised this kitten through me. My faith again was lifted to a higher dimension.

I didn't know the impact it had on my children. Just weeks later my eldest son Al Jr. came home from school and noticed his goldfish had jumped out of his fish bowl and had fallen to the floor and was laying there for quite a few hours until it died. My son picked it up from the floor and noticed its fins were stiff and its body quite dry. He took this fish and said, "In Jesus Christ name, I command this fish to live and not die" and dropped it in the fish bowl. When the fish touched the water immediately it came back to life and began to swim. When I came home from work my son told me, "Dad, look what Jesus did!" I replied, "What son? What did Jesus do for you?" "No,

Dad, not for me but for my fish! My fish was dead and I prayed and put him back in the water and he came back alive. Dad, I knew he would live because I saw how you prayed for Toby in Jesus name and he came back to life, so I said I could pray for my goldfish too." I was so excited my son's faith had increased to greater faith, because of what he saw his Dad do. Hallelujah!

A DRUNK MAN

I was invited by a precious Pastor to hold a healing service at his church in Tijuana, Baja California, Mexico. I prayed and asked God to send me. Remember, not all invitations which are given should be obliged. You must be released and sent by Him. You want to be sent by God because then He will equip you with everything you will need for them. When God calls us, He equips, provides, qualifies and enables us. In Hebrew 13:21 *"equip you with everything good for doing his will, and may He work in us what is pleasing to Him, through Jesus Christ, to whom be glory for ever and ever. Amen."* I have learned the hard way through my journey of thirty years of ministry, all doors must be opened by God alone.

I arrived at the church and began to pray before the service. I prayed to God thanking Him for allowing me to walk under His Glory. I came against any delay, derailing, and destruction which might want to dilute the service. I applied the blood of Jesus on me and on the congregation to not receive any backlash or retaliation, from that which I would come against. While praying I heard the orchestra playing and the most beautiful songs in Spanish being sung by the choir. The atmosphere was being transformed and the ambience of the sanctuary was Holy. I walked in and raised my hands to the King of kings and the Lord of lords. There were so many wonderful people worshiping God and I even saw children who had their eyes closed and their hands raised to our God of the universe. I was introduced and I began to welcome the Holy Spirit into the place. I began to teach, preach, and lay hands on the sick.

There were so many creative and regenerative miracles that night. I will always remember this sweet little boy about eight years of age, who was in the front row. He had on thick, black rimmed glasses with lenses which looked like the bottom of a coca-cola soda bottle. He kept on calling on Jesus for the healing of his eyes. As the night progressed, this little boy just came up to me and said, "Please Prophet Al, have God heal my eyes!". I said, "Please remove your glasses." I saw he was myopic. He couldn't see close and was almost blind. As I asked him to look at me he turned towards me with the help of my guiding hand and with crocodile tears running down his cheeks, he looked up and I noticed he was extremely cross-eyed, too. Not only was he not able to see very well, but his eyeballs both pulled close towards his nose. I told him, "Son you don't have to worry, I know a God. God is going to heal you tonight." He placed his small arms around me and held tight. I knew he believed. I blew in the name of Jesus Christ in his eyes (Charis Pneuma), the breath of God, and he began to weep. I gave him a Bible and asked him to read it. Without glasses and with a small print Bible, this little boy began to read the Word of God and the church stood to their feet and with a roar, they were thanking God for this little boy's miracle. I held him and said to everyone, "Yo se de un Dios!", I know a God!

There were many miracles and healing that night but, while I was praying, I heard one of the ushers saying to someone, "Stop you can't go down to the altar. Are you kidding me? Get out," he said! "You're drunk and you smell terrible! Go on get out!" Immediately, I stopped the service and called out for that man to be brought to the altar. Everyone was stunned that I wanted to talk to this drunken man. When he stood in front of me, I realized this man reeked of human waste and smelled of liquor. He told me, "Please tell God for me, I am sorry and if He can heal me." I saw a man who was desperate and needed God's love. Even though there was a tube coming out from under the hem of his pants which flowed with body fluids and excrement, I came close and held him and kissed his forehead and said, "The Lord loves you and wants to forgive you and heal you. You are God's son!." He began to weep as he echoed the sinners prayer, completely sober. As I prayed for him, he fell under the power of God. Two ushers took him by the arm and escorted him to the back of the church.

The following day this man came back to our next service. But, this time he was bathed, cleaned-clothed and sober. He seemed to be so excited because he said he had a testimony. That previous night, he went home, removed his pants and shirt and fell on his bed and slept like a baby. When he woke up the next morning, he rubbed his eyes and yawned. He got up and realized he had received his miracle. As he stood up from his bed the tube that protruded out of his stomach and colon were on the floor. He looked at his stomach which previously had a hole the size of a quarter, which was surgically placed there by the doctor to help accommodate his bodily functions. His stomach had no hole.... he was miraculously healed. Thank you Jesus! I learned because of having the compassion of God's people and the passion to have God heal through me, I went past my senses and allowed God to perform His miracles. Hallelujah!

The bible tells us not only Jesus but others have raised the dead, like Elijah resurrected the son of the widow from Zarephath. In 1 Kings 17:17-24 *"Now it happened after these things that the son of the woman who owned the house became sick. And his sickness was so serious that there was no breath left in him. So she said to Elijah, "What have I to do with you, O man of God? Have you come to me to bring my sin to remembrance, and to kill my son?" And he said to her, "Give me your son." So he took him out of her arms and carried him to the upper room where he was staying, and laid him on his own bed. Then he cried out to the Lord and said, "O Lord my God, have You also brought tragedy on the widow with whom I lodge, by killing her son?" And he stretched himself out on the child three times, and cried out to the Lord and said, "O lord my God, I pray, let this child's soul come back to him." Then the Lord heard the voice of Elijah; and the soul of the child came back to him, and he revived. Then the woman said to Elijah, "Now by this I know that you are a man of God, and that the word of the Lord in your mouth is the truth."*

The Bible accounts for many others like;

1. Elisha raised the son of the Shunammite woman from the dead.   (2 Kings 4:32-35)

2. A man was raised from the dead when his body touched Elisha's bones. (2 kings 13:20,21)

3. Many saints rose from the dead at the resurrection of Jesus. (Matt. 27:50-53)

4. Jesus rose from the dead. (Matt. 28:5-8)

5. Jesus raised the son of the widow of Nain from the dead. (Luke 7:11-15)

6. Jesus raised the daughter of Jairus from the dead. (Luke 8:41,42, 49-55)

7. Jesus raised Lazarus from the dead. (John 11:1-44)

8. Peter raised Dorcas from the dead. (Acts 9:36-41)

9. Eutychus was raised from the dead by Paul. (Acts 20:9,10)

I share these stories and testimonies with you to encourage you to begin to reach for the more of God. I know God can increase your faith. Your faith is not dependent on anything else but through your experiences with God. He is the one who will increase your faith to become great faith. Jesus tells us in John 14:12 *"Most assuredly, I say to you, he who believes in Me, the works that I do he will do also; and greater works than these he will do, because I go to My Father."*

Dear precious men and women of God, begin to believe God because He tells us most assuredly you will be able to raise the dead, heal the sick, cast out demons in His name. When the Lord tells us "MOST ASSUREDLY", that word means certainly, definitely, absolutely, without fail, and granted. Hold on to God's word and see that greater works shall you do than what Jesus did, in His name.

CHAPTER 4

HAPPY HOLY HANDS

When I invited Jesus into my heart, as my Lord and Savior, I was thirty-three years of age. I, at the time, was so desperate and felt alone, I needed Him. It was at the time I had just lost my grandmother. She died of a massive heart attack. I was devastated with her passing. My grieving for her was deep and I just couldn't find my way out of it. I battled deep depression and horrific panic attacks. I just couldn't bear not having her in my life. There was such a special bond between my grandmother and I. She was a powerfully gifted woman of God. She had an intimate relationship with God. She was a devout Seventh Day Adventist and attended her Saturday service faithfully. She was my liaison to God. I knew God through her. When I would ask her to pray for me, she would smile and say, "Of course!" After praying she would tell me. "Don't worry, I know a God." My faith was in her. If she would tell me she knew all was well, I would completely without any doubt believe her. When I was in a situation either it being a health issue or otherwise, she would always tell me with confidence "Don't worry my son, I know a God." Yes, my grandmother knew her God, and I was glad for it.

She would always use natural ways to teach me supernatural understandings. She once told me to look out her living room window. "Do you see that tree, the fig tree?" "Yes Grandma, I do." "Do you see all the leaves on that tree?" "Yes Grandma, I do." I was thinking, "Come on Grandma get to the point". Of course I would never tell her that because even though she was about four feet, eleven inches tall, she had a very heavy hand of correction. "Well then, do you see all the leaves are moving and swaying in the wind?" "Yes," I responded. "Not one leaf would move with the wind unless it is the will of God, my son. You're life is in the hands of the Lord. You have a great purpose of God in you. You"re life is not yours but His. You will be led by the Spirit of God, like those leaves move by the wind. The Holy Spirit will guide you and lead you by the ushering of the wind of the Lord. Remember that my son….just remember that."

My grandmother Eloise moved in the wisdom of the Lord. She knew how to place seed in me, to make me desire to know more of Him. She would say in her broken English, "Sing me a song." "What song do you want to hear?" I replied. I knew the one she would ask me to sing. It was always the same one. The one about the hat. There I would be, standing in front of her, a skinny ten year old boy singing "My hat, it has three corners, three corners has my hat, if my hat didn't have three corners, then it wouldn't be my hat." What a silly song that was, but she would smile and enjoy me singing it, over and over again. Oh, how I wish I could hear her ask me that again. I would sing that song to her anywhere and at any time. How I miss my little Grandma. She would always try to tell me about her Jesus and how I should sing for Him.

Well, I just wasn't going to have it. I would tell her she should sing to her God, but I was going to sing in the world and be a star. Years later I tried out for a Broadway Show and was given a leading role in Carousel . Can you imagine eighteen years old, a first time audition, and picked for the leading role? I was excited for the opportunity of a life time, but my father had me decline due to a family vacation which had been pre-planned and he had the last word. I called and released my part to the understudy. I was so devastated but was raised to honor my father's request. I would continue to sing in many places but a few times I sang at the John Wayne Airport Hotel Lounge. I was singing with a twelve-piece orchestra in one of the lounges next door to where Jose Feliciano was having his show. My show held standing room only and Frank Sinatra Jr. was in a front row seat. I was doing well and seemed to be going places with my career but something was missing. I missed my grandmother, her God, and my peace.

Becoming born again changed my life around. I was now seeing and experiencing a relationship with Jesus like the one my grandmother had. He was transforming me, healing me, and delivering me. I was no longer feeling empty inside, I had the King of kings and the Lord off lords inside of me. I was so in love with Jesus that I read the Bible and many books. I wanted to learn more about Him.

I was fortunate to be given a few books by Kenneth Hagin and Smith Wigglesworth. I would read them over and over again, I couldn't get enough of them. I would always ask the Lord to please use me in the way He used my grandmother, Kenneth Hagin and Smith Wigglesworth. I loved the stories of healing and the raising of the dead. Wow! Can you imagine being used by God to bring healing to the blind, opening the ears of the deaf, and seeing the lame begin to walk again. I made up my mind....that is what I wanted to do, lay hands on the sick and see them recover.

Before work around 7:00 am I would drive to the local Catholic Church, Saint Hilary, in Pico Rivera, California to pray and speak with Jesus. The doors of the church were always open, all night and all day, for those who wanted to come in to meditate or pray. I would find a seat and weep. I was almost always the only one there, in this big church. It was rather nice and quiet, and gave me a sense of holiness. I was able to get lost in Him. Just me and Jesus. In one of my mornings with the Lord, I asked Him to allow me to know Him in the way my grandmother knew Him. I wanted to be used by him. I prayed, "Lord please use me, let me travel to many nations proclaiming your word and demonstrating your power. Let your signs and wonders follow me wherever I go. I want to be used in a mighty way, which no man would be able to ever deny you exist. If you are going to use me like that, let me have power, your power in me. I am yours Lord, I give you my life." I thought for a moment and felt led to ask the Lord if He would give me a sign which would confirm my request to Him. "Your face Lord, let me see your face as confirmation."

I glanced at my watch and realized I had overstayed and needed to hurry to get to work on time. I went to work and diligently tried to do the best job I could as their Data Processing Manager. Five o'clock came and I was finished for the day, exhausted and very hungry. As I drove home I could only think of the dinner my wife Loretta had waiting for me.

Every evening before bedtime Loretta would tell me the tales of my three boys adventures that day, some were good reports, and some were not so good, more like bad ones, but a few times the evening would end up with me having to reprimand them…. ouch! But the night always ended up with me and Loretta kissing all three boys on their foreheads and tucking them in their beds. Loretta stayed up with me for a while and announced she was getting sleepy. She kissed me goodnight and went to bed. I was still a little wound up from my work demands that day and stayed up to unwind just a while longer. I watched a late night movie, slouched on my favorite chair in the den, and had all the lights switched off.

The den seemed to take on a new ambience when the lights were off as the television would cast its light and shadows all through the room. I sat and melted in my overstuffed chair and got comfortable. A few minutes had gone by and I heard a voice near my right ear which said, "Look this way". I looked around as I sat on my chair and thought maybe I was just thinking it or hearing it from the television. I dismissed it and continued to watch television. Again, I heard that voice telling me to look this way. I stood up and looked behind my chair and all around the room and didn't see anyone. I began talking to myself and said, "Am I losing it, I must be going crazy!" I returned to my seat closed my eyes and began to pray, "Satan get thee behind me in Jesus name." I quickly remembered the scripture in 2 Timothy 1:7 *"For God hath not given us the spirit of fear, but of power, and of love, and of a sound mind."* I slowly opened my eyes and continued to look around just a little more and I felt the coast was clear and said AMEN! A few minutes later, for the third time I heard that voice which was strong but yet gentle, bold but still loving saying "Come to me NOW!" I hurriedly got up and began to search my whole house. I yelled out..."Who are you? Where are you?" From the den, to the living room, past the dining room, down the hall and then to the only room left, the kitchen.

I entered the darkened kitchen and stopped in my tracks because the face of Jesus began to appear to the left of me, in front of the window curtain. His face was not made up of shadows and it wasn't a picture of Jesus; it was Him, flesh and blood, the face of the Lord. I looked at Him and He was looking back at me. I kept on looking at Him an I noticed He had olive skin and His beard was quite sparse. I could see His jawline was strong and chiseled, His nose wide and long. His brown hair was fine and wavy, cascading to His shoulders. He looked like a strong Hebrew man. Can you believe it? I was seeing Jesus right before my eyes. I looked into His eyes and fell in love with Him even more. His eyes were beautiful, not because of the color, which by the way were brown, it was the depth of love which emanated through them. They were comforting and at the same time so captivating. I saw His skin, His eyebrows, His lips…I saw the Lord.

After a few minutes I asked the Lord If He would allow me to have my wife see Him. I didn't really wait for His answer and began to run to our bedroom and woke her up. I said, "Loretta, wake up! Come with me. Let me show you something." She first said, "No….tell me first what it is." I said, "I can't. I wanted to tell her but I needed proof of what I had seen was real. It's not bad and really it's a good thing. Please come with me. Come on just trust me." So she got out of bed and we began to walk very close together, hand in hand, like Hansel and Gretel, the childhood storybook characters. Down the hall we went and because of my anticipation of my wanting her to see Jesus, every step we took, seemed longer. I wondered if she in fact did see Him would she be afraid. Loretta walked in the kitchen and quickly said "Honey look I see Jesus." "You really see Him Sweetheart, you really can see Him?" I asked. "Yes, yes I do." We both stood in front of our Savior, and we were overwhelmed by His presence. My wife, after a while broke the silence which hung in the air and commented, "Maybe this apparition is nothing more than the light of the moon, the street lamp casting its shadows against the ivy above our refrigerator and the shirts which have been laundered, hanging to dry." I knew what I was seeing. It was Jesus, it was God manifest in the flesh. I was seeing Jesus, God incarnate, real flesh, a real face. So in my mind I was thinking, just to appease my wife, I will tell her, "maybe," but truly I knew it wasn't so.

Before I was able to voice my appeasement, seven bolts of lightning shot through my body, entering through the top of my head. It was so strong I would double over and moan due to the pain it caused me. Loretta looked at me and asked me what was wrong. I couldn't speak, I was being over taken by these bolts of lightning. After the last bolt which shook my body the Lord audibly spoke to me. He said "You asked to see my face... I show you my face, and now you doubt me?" I felt as if I had betrayed Him. I felt as though I deeply disappointed Him. I was so afraid my God had chosen to extricate me from His presence, forever. "Please Lord, I am so sorry, forgive me! Please Lord, give me a second chance. I'm sorry! I will never doubt you again." I waited for His answer. I heard none. Through tears welling up in my eyes, I understood He had the right to do it because of what I did. I had betrayed Him. When I felt there was now no hope, I heard His beautiful, bold yet gentle voice, tell me, "Okay." He said, "Okay! " That was it, nothing less and nothing more. It was enough for me to be assured I was going to be used. He showed me His face. You might ask why did He only show you His face? Well, I asked Him if He was going to use me, confirm it by showing me His face. If he had shown me all of Him it could not correctly be confirmed to my request.

With my new found love and my sign of confirmation He was going to use me in healing all over the world, I began to lay hands on anyone who I could find. I wanted to see many people receive their healing and know God was alive and doing well. I would go to K-mart and walk around the store and find people who would be limping or have an ace bandage around their knee or elbow. It didn't matter, I wanted to pray and see God heal them and God did. So, there I was laying hands on the sick, at Bank of America, Disneyland, walking down the street, etc. I even praying for our neighborhood dogs and they too were getting healed. I found a living God and wanted everyone to experience Him. I was given the name "Happy Holy Hands." I don't know if it was a name the neighborhood gave me to mock me or a name of endearment but I didn't care much because my God was using me and I was loving it. What an honor it was to serve the Lord, and to see His word come alive through me.

As I walked through the neighborhood I greeted many neighbors hoping they would ask me how I was and when they did, I responded to them I am blessed and highly favored. I wanted them to ask why I answered that I was blessed and highly favored so I would have the opportunity to tell them it is because of Jesus. I would walk down the street every Wednesday at 6:30 pm to attend a Bible study carrying my Bible high under my arm, proudly displaying my sword to the world.

I never knew there was a woman who lived about six houses down from me who would peek through her living room window to see me walking down the street with my Bible under my arm singing and praising God. She would always say to herself, "He is always so happy and proud. But, he is a bit strange asking everyone as he walks if he can pray for them." I wonder where he goes every Wednesday at 6:30 pm? Her curiosity took the best of her and one day she decided to follow me and saw I was attending a Bible Study at South Ranchito Elementary School Auditorium, in the city of Pico Rivera. She came in and sat in the back and listened. She heard the pastor teaching us the Word of God and she saw there were other strange people like me who loved to sing to Jesus and raise their hands. She continued to come to the church and eventually became our friend and really got along well with my wife.

We were introduced to her children and husband but he wouldn't attend church often. On Sundays he would stay home and watch the ballgame, while his family would attend church. She would always request prayer for her husband, family, and her marriage. Both our children attended the same school so there was also another common bond between us. She noticed God was using me in healing and miracles. She spoke to Loretta, my wife, one afternoon at church, and told her she admired how I loved the Lord and how I was so open in my worship to Him. She couldn't believe the accuracy of the word of knowledge and the discerning of spirits which God had given me. She told my wife she was blessed to have a God-fearing husband.

Months had gone by and our relationship with our neighbor and her family was becoming much closer. She asked my wife if we would come and bless their home. When Loretta asked me, I said, "Yes absolutely." I knew I would have the opportunity to speak with her husband and hopefully pray with him. I wanted him to like me and maybe start coming to church more often.

When we arrived at their home, she greeted us with the warmest hug accompanied with a smile that seemed to go from ear to ear. She sat us down in her living room while her husband reached out his hand to me from across the coffee table thanking me and my wife for accepting their invitation. They were really gracious hosts. They continued to offer us delicious appetizers and beverages. I would glance at our hostess as she was sharing about their children. I noticed she seemed to be so happy as if she was expecting something, the way a child wakes up on Christmas morning. She knew God was going to do something big through me, for her.

We began to talk about our kids and sports, when out of nowhere, she asked if I could pray a blessing for their home. I saw in her eyes she was desperate, as if she were trying to tell me something but just couldn't. I replied, "Yes absolutely!" She didn't know, along with the others, I was feeling uncomfortable and spiritually discerning there was an entity, a demon, in this house. It was as if this home was controlled by a demonic force. The windows and doors were open but there was no wind coming through. Everything was still. There appeared to be no life in this home. I stood up and asked if I could have the liberty to walk around and pray and see what God would have me do. She quickly said, "Yes, please do," as she too, stood up with an expectancy. I began to pray, my wife agreeing with me in prayer. I walked around the living room and was led by the Spirit of the Lord, the Holy Ghost to enter the dining room. I stood there and through the gift of discerning of spirits, I saw a grotesque looking, big and tall demon cowering in the corner of the room. It knew I was there but was trying to hide. I told our hostess, "There is a demon in that corner of your room." She commented, "Really, are you sure?" I said, "Give me your hand and place it near this area...you will see." She reluctantly obliged me and reached out to feel. She yelled and said "It's as cold as ice right there," "Yes, that's the demon." I replied.

I told them both I wanted to tell them what I knew, but I would need their permission. I asked for them to send their children outside. While the children were leaving, I began to apply the blood of Jesus upon myself, my wife, and them too. I asked the husband, "When your wife is at church what do you do in this room?" He hesitantly said, "What do you mean?" I told him, "You are looking at books and movies in this room which are luring you to lust." He dropped his head and slowly nodded. I said, "I am not here to judge anyone, but to love you through your condition and this house cleansing. The demon which is hiding in the corner believes he has the right to be here. His name is lust." I asked them both to repent and ask forgiveness for anything they both could have done to open the door to this demon. I went over to the corner and declared, "In the name of Jesus I command you lust demon to remove yourself from this corner and leave this home, and never return." Instantly, it flew past me and the curtains flew up allowing passage through the open window. At the same time, she began to cough and dark grey smoke came out of her mouth. We were all taken aback for what had manifested.

I yelled from the top of my voice, "Father in the name of Jesus Isaiah 54:17 says *"No weapon that is formed against you shall prosper: and every tongue that shall rise against you in judgment you shall condemn. This is the heritage of the servants of the Lord, and their righteousness is of me, saith the Lord."* I continued *with* 1 John 4:4 *"Ye are of God, little children, and have overcome them; because greater is He that is in you, than he that is in the world."* We looked at each other and thanked the Lord for what He had done. It was an open heaven experience. We told them we had to leave now because we had another appointment we needed to meet. We hugged and said our goodbyes and walked out.

I sat in the car and thanked the Lord for using me. My wife looked at me and said, "God is really using you. You could really see that demon and command him to leave. I saw the curtain fly up as it left. I saw the smoke come out of her mouth." Loretta continued, "Sometimes you scare me. To wrestle with demons and cast them out, that's so supernatural." "I know," I replied, "That's exactly what the Bible tells us in Ephesians 6:12 *"For we wrestle not against flesh and blood, but against principalities, against powers, against the rulers of the darkness of this world, against spiritual wickedness in high places."* My wife was quite overwhelmed with what took place that day.

The next day this precious neighbor called me on the phone and was crying and trying to tell me something through her tears of joy. I only listened and said, "I will wait until you can find your composure." She started by thanking me over and over again. "You don't know what God really did through you. What God did in my home with that demon, even the smoke which came out of my mouth, only pales to what God did for me last night. I have to tell you! I have to glorify God, for what He did for me. You see, every night for ten years, this gorgeous naked handsome man would walk in my room and get on top of me and start making love to me which would turn into raping me. I would kick and try to push him off of me. He would turn into this hideous monster looking demon. I didn't tell my husband because of the guilt that I was being with another man. It wouldn't take no for an answer. I was so confused. I was being raped every night for ten years, Brother Al, ten years. I hurt my husband so badly because I could never completely abandon myself to him. He wanted to make love to me and I just wanted to have sex with him and get it over with. He didn't know what was happening to me every night for years. Until last night, Brother Al. I was able to make love with my husband. It was beautiful and intimate. My husband noticed my abandonment to him. He saw gentleness in my eyes for him.

You see, the demon you found in my dining room was my nighttime rapist, my lover, my monster. It held me in fear, I was in bondage to him. I couldn't get away, who could I have told? Who would have believed me? I knew if I told anyone they would accuse me of being crazy. I didn't want to lose my children or my marriage. I would think I would land up in a mental ward. That demon made me believe I had no way out, no options. He led me to believe I was his for life. That's why I asked your wife to have you come and bless my home. I was hoping you would see what I was going through, and you did. God used you and I am forever grateful for your obedience to Him and His gift in you. I love my husband, I love my marriage, I love the Lord." I told her, "God is so good and thank you for allowing me to be a part of your deliverance and breakthrough."

Once I had a visitation with the Lord for two and a half hours. Even though I have had many visitations with the Lord, this one proved to be one of the most influential concerning my ministry. The Lord told me whatever I come against will try to come against me. This is what happened after praying for my neighbor who was being raped by a demon for ten years. I cast him out of their house in the name of Jesus and told him he was not to come back. I knew this lust demon was mad at me but I didn't know he would retaliate. About a month had gone by from the deliverance of the lady when I heard knocking at my front door. The knocking continued and wouldn't stop. As I opened the door I found my brother's friend looking at me cross-eyed. He was inebriated. He was so drunk he slurred and couldn't walk. I grabbed him and carried him into my house. I said, "How did you find my house?" Because I knew he didn't know where I lived. He kept on saying, "I'm sorry please forgive me." "You don't have to ask me for forgiveness, ask the Lord. I don't know what you have done but Jesus paid the price for your sins." He became incoherent and fell right in front of me on my living room floor having his back facing me.

I knelt down behind him and began to pray for him. All of a sudden his head turned back at me but his body still lay motionless. It looked bizarre, almost like what Linda Blaire's character did in The Exorcist. A demon began to speak through his mouth and said, "I know who you are. Remember the lady down the street? You demanded me to leave her house. You cast me out!" His voice was not this young man's. It was a voice which was deep, and guttural, which resonated in the room. This demon was mad at me, he told me, "You have no power! and I said, "You're right I don't have any power, but the God in me does." He retorted "You can't touch me!" Not a bit shaken I said "You're right again. I can't touch you but God through me can." So the demon growled and tried to curse me. With authority I said to him, "Greater is He that is in me, than he that is in the world. I command you to leave. You cannot stay in this man. Leave now!" I applied the blood of the lamb on this young man.

My wife and eldest son heard that hideous growl and came into the room to investigate. When they recognized it was coming out of my brother's friend's mouth, they both quickly turned and left the room. I said to the demon, "Get out now!" With a big, vociferous voice it began to scream out and left. This young man opened his eyes and saw he was on the floor. He said, "Al, what am I doing here? What is going on? Whose house is this?" I helped him up and noticed he was no longer drunk. He was completely sober. I decided not to tell him about the demon who was using him to scare me. I didn't tell him it was that demon who guided him to my house. I just said to him, "Hey, it's nice to see you and I'm glad you're alright." Again, I thank God for His protection and power. I'm glad I know a God!

CHAPTER 5

MAYAN GODS

O ne year my wife and I took a trip down south to Cancun, Mexico. This city is in southeastern Mexico, located on the northeast coast of the Yucatan Peninsula in the Mexican state of Quintana Roo. We had invited a few precious friends to travel with us, and together, we enjoyed learning about the culture of the Mayans, and of their cuisine. I had heard of the pristine blue clear waters and white sands the shores of Cancun offered, and it goes without saying, their beaches are some of the best I have seen in the world. We visited two Mayan Pyramids, Tulum and Chichen Itza. These two archeological sites proved to be quite culturally interesting and architecturally magnificent.

I rented a van for the day to travel to the pyramid locations. I was elected to drive, which by the way, I love doing. But, before leaving from our hotel room to begin our excursion, I asked everyone, "Lets pray for safe travel." We formed a circle and held hands. I prayed this prayer. "Father in the name of Jesus, we come before you. I bless your name and give you honor. Today, as we travel through the jungle, please keep us safe. I charge warrior angels to protect us. I apply the blood of Jesus, from the crowns of our heads to the soles of our feet. I call on traveling mercy to be about us." I continued the prayer saying, "I come against any backlash or retaliation, in the name of Jesus. All witchcraft must not touch or harm any of us. I come against all perversion and I call out serpentine demons, and phallic demons, in the name of Jesus Christ." After praying that prayer everyone said "Amen" and looked at me with a look of concern. They began questioning me why I would pray against such demons, I said to them "I'm not really sure, but that's what came out of my mouth." I too, began to question my prayer. But, again, I know a God.

We began to prepare ourselves for the journey of our lifetime, our jungle adventure. I got in the van and yelled out, "Find your seat for we are headed out now to find secret treasures and the Lost Ark of the Covenant." Everyone laughed and I commented, "Maybe there's too much Doctor Indiana Jones in me or too many times seeing that movie." Anyway we found our map and began to drive. As I drove on a two lane jungle highway headed to our destination, someone asked me if I knew a little about Chichen Itza and its history. I said, "I know some history." I told him Chichen Itza is in the southeastern part of Mexico. It is one of the most important ancient Mayan cities. The most impressive building in Chichen Itza is known as El Castillo or Kukulcan Pyramid, but the whole city is a true wonder of pre-Columbian architecture. I told them at the ruins we are going to see their great ball court, The Temple of the Warriors, El Caracol, Las Monjas, and many more structures including the Cenote Sagrado (Sacred Cenote), a natural sinkhole which was a place of pilgrimage where ancient Mayans conducted sacrifices. Ancient Mayans believed the rain god chaak resided in caves and natural wells called cenotes. Mayan farmers today in Mexico's parched Yucatan still appeal to chaak for the gift of rain. The Mayan people would sacrifice virgin maidens and great treasures like gold and jewels to their rain god.

The drive was so peaceful, picturesque, and undeniably beautiful. The Yucatan jungle grew so thickly dense which created a wall of flora which mounted up to about forty to fifty feet on both sides of the road. The canopy of tall palms and trees were majestic and enchanting. We stopped a few times to speak to some of the most colorfully clothed indigenous Mayan Indians who were stationed alongside the road. They were selling their vibrant hammocks, baskets and jewelry. The barbecued meats gave off such a delicious aroma and grilled seasoned corn on the cob bathed in butter almost won me over. There were many exotic fruits being offered for sale too. A few of my friends ate but I was a little hesitant. I didn't want to eat some food which would not agree with my stomach. You see, jungles don't have bathrooms, I'm sure you get my point. So I was stuck with eating day old pretzels and stale chips.

We thanked the vendors and got back in the van to continue our trek. We finally arrived at our archeological site and realized we had already traveled for about two and half hours. We parked in a makeshift dirt parking lot and got out and stretched our legs. We were happy to have arrived. We had finished our last bottles of water knowing we needed to purchase more. It was about 105 degrees and we were perspiring heavily. It was scorching hot but even that didn't stop our excitement for what was ahead. We were going to see the Mayan Ruins. We felt as if we were walking back in time. Walking with excitement and anticipation for what we were just about to see, allowed us not to be cognizant that the road we were walking was long, the sun was hot atop our heads, and our foreheads and backs were dripping with perspiration. Because of the sun Mayan vendors had pitched canopies to cover themselves, as well as the buyers, to display their wonderfully crafted baskets and hammocks. I saw many of the elderly women were making Mayan dolls out of cloth, with many brightly colored ribbons and beads. Most of the vendors were selling various flutes, whistles, and smoking pipes which were made of different materials, like onyx, turquoise, and assorted woods. I picked up one of these pieces of art and admired it. I appreciated the time and patience it must have taken to display the craftsmanship of the Mayan artisans of today and of their ancestors. But, I was surprised to see the majority of the carved figurines and musical instruments were carved on one side to resemble the male genitalia. It was amazing to see everything which was made seemed to glorify the male genitalia. I quickly put the art piece back in its place and thanked the vendor.

We continued our walk towards the entrance of the ancient Chichen Itza Mayan city, and as we approached the entrance, standing tall were massive and strong walls. From the north, south, east, and west, the walls proudly surrounded and protected what lay within. We were greeted by a Mayan tour guide, who had a brilliant contagious smile and he began to teach us about the history and culture of the Mayan people. We were educated on how the people lived, how they worked, and even their source of entertainment. It was all so interesting. We began to feel exhausted due to the walk and heat. The tour ended at the Sacred Cenote (water sink hole) which was quite large. We were told of the many human virgin sacrifices, gold, and jewels which had been thrown into this Cenote. My wife, Pastor Loretta and others in our group were beginning to get overheated. I was very concerned and told them we must be careful not to get a heatstroke. They all began to find shade the trees offered to try to cool down their overheated bodies.

I saw a small store in the back against the inside of the wall. A young man was in front of the store sweeping the dirt and sprinkling water on it. They were selling bottles of cold water and snacks. I noticed as I neared the store the young man was using a glass soda bottle, corked with a makeshift metal spigot with a few holes on it. I found it funny in what this man was doing so I told him, "Porque estas bariendo tierra, tierra es tierra?" (Why are you sweeping dirt, when dirt is dirt?) He laughed with me and then sprinkled a few drops of water to settle the dust. I told him he needed to wet the ground more than just a few drops to accomplish the task. He looked at me and said, "They were in a great drought and couldn't use too much water." I told him to forgive me for being so rude in trying to have you use more water. "Oh, Don't worry Sir, I know you were playing around with me, but this is a serious matter to my family and the Mayan people. We have been in a drought now for three years."

With concern I said, "I'm sorry for you and the villagers in the region." His reply was, "It's okay because we are all praying for rain to come down quickly." "Whom do you pray to?" I asked. "To our rain god chaak." He replied. "Do you mean for three years you have petitioned your god to help you have rain?" He said "Yes!" "Well," I said, "Your god must be either deaf or doesn't care. What if I pray to my God, the God of Abraham, Isaac, and Jacob? It is my Father who sent His son Jesus to save me and help me. He will hear my petition on your behalf. He will bring down rain. If you see rain coming down from this sky today will you ask my God to be your God and Jesus Christ to be your Savior?" He said, "If I see rain today....yes!"

Remember, it hadn't rained for over three years. It was around 105 degrees and the day had the bluest skies you could ever see, and not one cloud could be seen. Now, due to my proclamation, many people including our team were gathering around me and the young man. Some I could tell by their faces and gestures they thought I was plain crazy, while others believed my words with anticipation. They must have thought I was a vociferous lunatic because all the natural facts would undoubtedly prove me wrong. But, there I stood with my right hand raised towards the sky and praying to my God saying; "Father God, in the name of Jesus Christ of Nazareth, I come before You. This young Mayan man needs to see this miracle of rain. He must know I know a God, a living God who hears His sons and daughters. This young Mayan man will be used as a gateway to many Mayan people who will come to know you as their Lord and Savior. I pray this according to your word found in Mathew 18:19-20 which reads "*Again, I tell you that if two of you on earth agree about anything you ask for, it will be done for you by my Father in heaven. For where two or three come together in my name, there am I with them'.*" and before I was able to say Amen......rain began to fall, a strong rain, no clouds, just God!

People began to cry out, others raised their hands. The young Mayan man was on his knees, weeping for joy. He asked me, "Please introduce me to your God." I asked him to repent of all his sins and invite the Lord Jesus Christ into his heart, allowing Jesus to become his Lord and Savior. This young Mayan man repented and invited the Lord Jesus into his heart, becoming born again. I was overwhelmed with God's miracle because this young man would become the gateway to many of his people's salvation.

We began to dance in the mud and shout from the top of our lungs proclaiming and thanking our precious Lord for this most creative miracle. This Jesus experience reminded me of the experience Elijah had with God. In 1 Kings 17:1, *"Now Elijah the Tishbite was a prophet from the settlers in Gilead. "I serve the Lord, the God of Israel," Elijah said to Ahab. "As surely as the Lord lives, no rain or dew will fall during the these years unless I command it."* What was God doing when He told Elijah to tell King Ahab, the most wicked king that ever squatted upon the throne of Israel, there would be no rain for these years? We understand through script in James 5:17 rain did not fall for three years and six months. You must understand he was married to a wretchedly evil woman named Jezebel. She was the daughter of the king of Zidon. They were all ardent Baal worshipers. God through Elijah was coming against their god. He was denouncing their false god Baal.

The Baal worshippers believed he was seen in the thunderheads and in the rain that fell. They would perform their immoral acts of sacrifice atop many hills to him to see rain begin to fall. So we see God proved to be God of all and most powerful of all. It didn't rain for over three years until God spoke to Elijah to command rain to fall, again. We see in 1 Kings 18:44 God lifted the curse which was upon the people who worshiped Baal. Elijah sent out a messenger to see a cloud as small as a man's hand and after the seventh attempt, it stormed. God proved through Elijah then, as he proved through me in this generation, He is God. He can defy science. He encourages us to go beyond our understanding and our own strengths to allow ourselves and many around our circle of influence to know we know a God. Amen and Amen!

As the sun began to set, the moon proudly took its place and cast its light on the ruins. The pyramids cast shadows from the light of the moon on its corners that resembled a serpent slithering down from the pinnacle of the pyramid, It was constructed in that way to cast shadows forming a snake in allegiance to a serpentine god named kukulkan, which is their plumed serpent also known as their feathered serpent. Their god closely related to kukulkan is god q'uq'umatz of the k'iche' maya.

A light show was offered with many colors to bring a festive ambience against the pyramids which canopied what seemed to be a rather eerie night transforming it to beauty. There were hundreds of people who found their places to view the light show. Throughout the pyramid light show I felt a demonic heaviness surround me. I continued to pray against these demons. I questioned many of my team, "Can you feel the oppression of demonic warfare in this place?" They replied, "We have been sensing it for a while." We all covered ourselves with the blood protection of Jesus and noticed it was getting late and quite dark in the midst of the Yucatan Jungle, so we decided to return to our hotel.

We walked back to our parked van and welcomed the soft seats which awaited us. I began to drive back through the same two lane highway, and was secretly thankful to be headed back. I had felt a slight oppression sporadically during the day. It was as if something was hovering over me. I would cover myself with the blood of the Jesus, but still sensed a heaviness in the air which seemed to increase in strength as darkness continued to fall. We had driven for about twenty minutes while singing songs, and I noticed in front of us a tree had fallen. It was about thirty feet tall and fell in front of the van, from the right, which suddenly blocked the road. I had to think quickly to avoid hitting it, so I swerved to the left. We were safe and I said, "All is well." Though they don't have any streets with lights, the moonlight was bright enough to allow me enough time to see it and turn. I thanked Jesus and we continued on our way, all unharmed. About thirty minutes later, a tree fell to my right and it tried to block me from continuing our return home. I swerved to the right this time and said "Wow, That was a close call!" I asked everyone to pray for God's traveling mercy. That was now two trees which tried to stop me in the middle of the jungle. I gathered my composure and continued to drive, but now with some apprehension. I immediately began to pray in my heavenly language, as the others were doing, also. "We are about half way now.....it's going to be okay!" My eyes were glued to the road. I would look to the right and to the left trying to see as far as I could, to give me time to maneuver the van out of danger if I had to again.

It seemed like an hour had passed when I saw this white dot coming towards us which seemed to get bigger and bigger as we approached. From the size of a baseball it grew to about the size of a beach ball. I said, "What is that?" I noticed it was a big white owl. It seemed to be flying straight towards us. This big white owl didn't veer off but slammed head-on into the right headlight. Many in the van yelled out to me, "Watch out!" but we both, this owl and I were going too fast to be able to turn. After the hit, I slowed down and stopped beside the road. I got out of the van and checked to see what damage the owl had caused. There was no sign of blood, no feathers, no dents and the headlight was not broken. How could that be? Where was the owl? I walked around the van and down the road and there was no owl to be found. I ran back to the van and said, "Come on let's go!" We all had calmed down after about thirty minutes of silence. We started talking again and telling jokes about the owl. I looked at my watch and told everyone we only had about a half hour more to go and we would be in our warm, comfortable beds. When out of nowhere a snake fell from the sky and hit the bottom of the windshield. This snake was so long and thick as it stretched across the van. I could not see the head or the tail for it was longer than the width of the van. It rolled up the windshield, across the top of the van....and we could hear it rolling passed us. Big, thick, long, and heavy. I pressed down on the gas pedal and it rolled off. I don't know what you would do, but we all were praying hard and loud. How can a snake fall on our van like that when there were no vines or limbs from trees that would have grown over the road?

The Lord began to remind me of my prayer I prayed before we started our excursion. I said to everyone in the van, "Remember, I prayed against witchcraft, serpentine snake demons, and even a phallic demon?" They all said, "Yes, We remember." I began to explain to them saying, "Don't you see? All those flutes and pipes were carved into male genitalia and even some of the ruins had the male genitalia carved on walls? Remember we walked in through the entrance and right in front of us was a tall carved granite male genitalia pillar? We also saw how they worship their snake god. Right? Don't you see? The Lord told me what I come against will try to come against me. Don't you see it? Satan and his cohorts wanted to retaliate! The witches, warlocks, and shamans were angry at me because I defied their gods, their snake god kukulkan , their rain god chaak. Even the worship of the male genitalia which is their god of fertility and manhood is also chaak."

The road trip back home to our hotel was definitely a backlash, and retaliation by every demon, and satan's cohorts which I came against. God proved to everyone He is the Alpha and the Omega, the beginning and the end. He tells us there will be no other god before Him. God is the one who is, who was and who is to come, the Almighty. I thank Him for who He is in my life. As I have traveled all over the world I tell everyone......I still know a God!

CHAPTER 6

MY OFFICE

have learned throughout my journey with the Lord, He continues to teach me who He is, in me. I have realized my learning is to prepare me for His purpose. I have failed many times in my testings throughout the years. I have had difficult times in the valleys. I couldn't see what I could learn from a disappointment, discouragement, or a door not wanting to open for me. When one opened, I felt I wasn't ready or conceivably qualified for. I was ultimately learning to die to self. It was knowing God's choosing and God's elections were perfect for purpose. My failure to choose what is truly God's perfect will in my life starts with me and ends with me. I had to recognize the importance of my obedience to Him, my God, the author and finisher, my beginning and my end.

Through my God experiences and testings, I have learned, and I am continuing to learn my reasoning, my intellect, my understanding and my emotion only derails and delays the God purpose in me. How am I going to be any good for God? How can I be qualified to go into the depths and dimensions of God? The Bible tells us in 1 Corinthians 2:10 *"The Spirit of God searches all things, even the deep things of God"*. I cried out, "I want the deep, Lord. I want the deep!" I love it when Psalms 42:7 reads *"Deep calleth unto deep at the noise of thy waterspouts: all thy waves and thy billows are gone over me."*

The Lord continues to call us closer to Him. He continues to teach me to listen to His still small voice. When God instructed Elijah to stand on the mountain in His presence, He sent a mighty wind which broke the rocks in pieces. He sent an earthquake and a fire, but His voice was in none of them. Afterwards, the Lord spoke to Elijah in the still small voice, a gentle whisper. God began to teach me to listen to His still small voice. I had to learn to trust Him enough to be still and allow God to be God in all my life.

You might ask me why would God continue to test us? What's the point of it all? I know at times, I, too, have asked the same questions because of being uncomfortable in a situation, or not liking what I am going through. Let me give you a word of advice to help jumpstart you to victory in Him...Jesus always wins and His purpose in you will always prevail. Proverbs 19:21, *"Many are the plans in a person's heart, but it is the Lord's purpose that will prevail."* In other words, God will have you accomplish His purpose through two different roads....the easy way or the hard. I know, I've traveled them both.

I didn't know God would use my office as His room of instruction to allow me to be able to go into the deep. I didn't know He would test my obedience and trust in Him, allowing me to enter into His realm, into His dimensions, into the deep with Him...the Supernatural. I will share some of my tests in my office and pray it will encourage your want for more of Him.

I was blessed to have a large office. It was able to house a seating area, my desk and a conference table which comfortably seated eight people. Many times I was able to fit up to twelve people in my office and still not feel cramped. There were no windows in my office and it was located on the second floor of our building.

Our Church, called Desert Bloom Ministries was located in Whittier, California. We were experiencing great moves of God and signs and wonders were always present in every service. I was and still am so thankful to God for allowing me to be under His Glory. I attributed our open-heaven experiences to our prayer warriors collectively, as well as, my personal prayers in my office. I would love to pray in my office with all the lights switched off. Praying in my darkened office always allowed me to go deep in Him. It was as though I was separated from everything and everyone. When I would close my door, I was His, and He was all mine. Many times I would start my time with God singing a worship song to Him. My favorite song to sing before interceding was "I Am Yours." The words were so close to my heart it would always bring me to the place of intimacy with my Jesus. For those who may not know this song and for the benefit of understanding, this is how I readied my heart for Him.

I am yours, I am yours.
I've been bought with life so precious.
I am new, so brand new, In you my Jesus.

I am yours, yes I'm yours,
and you hold my life in your hands
and when I hear your Spirit call...calling me....
I will follow, yes I will follow
because I'm yours.

It is a song of abandonment. It is a song of my love for Him. It was my heart's cry to my Lord, my God, my Love.

I would always ask for forgiveness in whatever I had done to displease or offend Him. I would let Him know He had all of me. I would pray, "I give you my mind, my eyes, my mouth, my ears, my heart, my hands, and my feet. I give you all of me." I would give Him my will, so He would be able to go past my will and have His will be done in me. Yes, I would say, "Yes dear Lord, "Have your way with me."

BLIND EYES

I can remember one night, as I sang and wept, I abandoned myself to Him and continued to pray in the Spirit for a while when something happened which truly frightened me. My hands were raised to Him and I was praying when my eyes began to go blind, as if dark black oil was filling up my eyes. I began to tremble with fear. I said, "Oh, "My God I must be bleeding in my eyes...maybe an eye aneurism." I don't know if that is altogether medically or physically possible, but that was what I thought. I quickly opened my eyes and cried out to God to help me in my condition. With my eyes open, trying to see in the dark, I was fine. No blindness, no pain...what happened? I began to massage my eyes to feel if there was any blood which had seeped out of my eyelids, but, I was fine.

Standing in the dark covering my eyes with my hands, I thought, what is this eye thing? Was it a God thing? What if He was going to show me something great and supernatural...and I stopped it because of fear. Now I was afraid I might have displeased the Lord or offended Him, because I was afraid. I collected myself and found all the composure I could muster up and asked God to forgive me, if what I experienced was of Him, and I didn't realize it, forgive me. I told Him, "Please Lord if this was you...please give me a second chance." I reminded Him His word tells me in John 1:9 *"If we confess our sins, he is faithful and just to forgive us all our sins, and to cleanse us from all unrighteousness"*. I said, "Please Lord give me a second chance. I know You are a God of a second chance. Jonah cried out to You by reason of his affliction and You heard him. You took him out of the belly of the whale. You gave him a second chance. Please give me a second chance." I didn't hear His still small voice but I, in faith just closed my eyes again and said, "I am ready, Lord." Instantly my eyes began to fill up with a blackness, but this time I wasn't afraid, I welcomed it, because I knew it was God. I kept on praying and telling Him I loved Him and thanked Him for giving me a second chance. My eyes filled up completely and like before I was totally blind. I didn't care, I had Him, I had His presence. I felt Him around me, I felt Him in me. He was with me!

I opened my eyes and couldn't see the walls, or my hands which were positioned right in front of my eyes, nothing but black. I felt His warmth cascade down my head flowing throughout my body and felt such a peace. The peace He speaks of that passes all understanding. (Philippians 4:7) In the natural, I should have been worried. My mind told me to call 911 for help. But the Comforter the Holy Spirit who resides in me continued to calm me and assured me it was God. It was well with my soul. I eventually looked up towards heaven. My office seemed to become animated. Nothing seemed more important than what I was seeing above me. The ceiling of my office was completely gone. What appeared before my eyes was a very dark, jet black sky, likened to a black velvet backdrop. I stared at this for a few minutes and was overwhelmed. I saw stars which were being positioned in the sky. They would come into view one by one, some far away and others near. They looked like brilliant diamonds twinkling. I know it seems so unreal but this is what I physically saw. It was an open vision. Thousands upon thousands of stars lit up the sky and all the stars twinkled individually. I stood in amazement telling God how grateful I was for this supernatural open vision.

All of a sudden high above a red ribbon appeared and began to fall very slowly, in the way a light feather would float to the ground. It continued to fall coming closer but still too far to recognize it to be anything other than a long red ribbon. Eventually, it was only about a hundred feet away from my reach. I realized it wasn't a ribbon at all. It was dancing angels holding hands together in a line, some with instruments I knew not of. They began to rejoice and play their instruments and fly all around the top of my office. I said, "Wow...how great is this?" Even though I knew I was seeing all this, I wanted to have proof of what my eyes where seeing. Someone else to see what I was seeing. I walked slowly to my door and opened it to call my wife and one of my pastors to come pray with me. As they entered my darkened office to pray with me, as they had many times before, nothing seemed unusual to them. Moments later one of them said, "Pastor Al, "Your ceiling is gone and I see a black sky like velvet with stars like diamonds." I said, "Yes...and what else?" With amazement she declared, "There are a lot of angels dancing!" I asked my wife Pastor Loretta, "What do you see?" She replied, "Exactly the same thing. Five pastors altogether came in and without telling them or suggesting for them to see anything, they each saw the angels. My God! We were so under God's open heaven.

I later realized God was gifting us with great faith. He was having me see there are other dimensions in Him. He was giving me my experience to believe for more. It was the same experiences so many men and women of old had experienced. Luke 24:22-23 reads *"And moreover, some women of our company astounded us and drove us out of our senses. They were at the tomb early (in the morning) but did not find His body; and they returned saying that they had (even) seen a vision of angels, who said that He was alive!"* Paul had a vision in the night in Acts 16:9. Apostle John, in the book of Revelation tells us he had open visions. He saw heaven. He saw a multitude which no one could number, of all nations, tribes, peoples, and tongues standing around the throne and before the lamb, clothed in white robes, with palm branches in their hands. God wants to enlighten our eyes. He wants to take us deeper, but will we allow Him to?

AGAINST THE WALL

In that same office, I was alone praying to God. I was against the wall in the dark. My forehead, chest and hands were against the wall, as I began to pray to Him. I was having such a wonderful time talking to Him, giving Him my petitions and supplications. I was adoring Him and thanking Him. I got so lost in my prayer to Him time seemed not to be a part of me or the room. As I prayed to Him, the Lord spoke to me and asked me to bow before Him. I replied, "Yes, My Lord, I will bow before you but let me please finish my intercession, and my prayer time with you." I was so enjoying His presence. He said again but just a little bit stronger, "Bow down to Me," and again I said, "Of course I will, but just give me a moment and I will bow." He said with yet a stronger voice, "BOW TO ME NOW!" I was so startled at the intensity of His voice I immediately bowed my head and realized my hands were still on the wall but my head had passed through the wall. I quickly pushed back my head and didn't know what to think. That is when the Lord taught me something so pivotal, so paramount to propel me to a higher faith in Him. I just went through the wall! How can that be? I was dumbfounded. I had many questions and I knew He would have all the answers. He said to me, "Yes my son, your head went through the wall, I allowed it. "I AM" teaching you I am above   science. "I AM" the one who created all things. I commanded every molecule and atom to align themselves to accept your atoms to allow your head to pass through them. Everything bows before me, even the atoms, protons, and molecules…everything. You must learn to trust Me completely. You must understand with the natural eye you see a wall but a wall isn't there until I tell you it is. "I AM" teaching you, my son, to believe the things that are not as though they were." I am reminded in Hebrews 11:1 it reads *"Now faith is the confidence that what we hope for will actually happen. It gives us assurance about things we cannot see."* I was beginning to understand God who created all, knows all, and is in all. He can have a rock spew out water, as He did for Moses. He taught many of His disciples how He is a supernatural God and moves in the dimensions of the supernatural.

Later on that night I began to remember so many stories in the Bible where Jesus displayed the supernatural by defying science. I closed my eyes as I lay in bed. I couldn't sleep. I mean think about it, I went through a wall! Right? I mean that doesn't happen too often nor happen at all, but, it happened. Wow! In my mind I saw Peter walking on water as the Lord beckoned him to come towards Him. I was just about to fall asleep when I thanked the Lord for this experience and told Him "I am not afraid, please show me more." I was like a child in a candy store. He opened my eyes to the supernatural and now I wanted to stay there. What was next? What will He teach me, next? I found myself smiling as I drifted off to asleep.

A FLAME OF FIRE

Again, in my office, I would invite some of my intercessors to come pray with me. On this particular night, I invited around twelve of my precious intercessors. Some were associate pastors while others were powerfully gifted prayer warriors. They knew already I prayed in the dark. One by one they entered into my office and found their place to stand. This became their tent of meeting, the place where they would anticipate to meet with Jesus. I had asked them to agree with me in Jesus name that God would give us the heart of an intercessor. I knew if we began intercession in our own might, or in our own power, we would never reach the place where God was. Years before, the Holy Spirit gave me a secret of how to enter His secret place, the holy place where He is, and it was through His word in Zechariah 4:6 *"Then he answered and spake unto me, saying, this is the word of the Lord unto Zerubbabel, saying, Not by might, nor by power, but by my Spirit, saith the Lord of hosts."* We had to enter in through His Spirit. The Holy Spirit, which is the Spirit of God, would lead us to pray, how to pray, and what to pray. He taught me to listen while praying in my heavenly language and His instruction would come. There were times I would hear words in my spirit to war and come against something, or audibly hear His still small voice asking me to be still and meditate in Him. Again, I realized prayer must be accompanied by faith, faith in Him. Praying in my heavenly language made me rest in Him and trust that the Spirit of the Lord was making perfect and specific intercession on my behalf. Romans 8:26-27 reads *"Likewise the Spirit also helps in our weaknesses. For we do not know what we should pray for as we ought, but the Spirit Himself makes intercession for us with groaning which cannot be uttered. Now He who searches the hearts knows what the mind of the Spirit is, because He makes intercession for the saints according to the will of God."*

As they agreed with me for the Spirit of God to help us find God's perfect will in showing us who to pray for or what to pray for, we began to pray in our heavenly language. I could hear in the room the sound of many voices becoming one. It was the sound which seemed to unite our hearts. It was no longer our might, or our power, it was His Spirit in us which took over. We found ourselves flowing in God's river of intercession. Truly, the oneness of this upper room intercession, was as the voice of many waters, as the voice of mighty thunderings, as the voice of a great multitude, as the voice of the Lord. In the book of Psalms 29:3-4 it reads *"The voice of the Lord is upon the waters, the God of Glory thundereth the Lord is upon many waters. the voice of the Lord is powerful the voice of the Lord is full of majesty."* His presence was felt; His Shekinah Glory was seen. (Shekinah means in Hebrew "He caused to dwell). We were having a divine visitation of the presence of the Lord God on this earth, here in my office.

I asked God through the name of His Son Jesus to allow my intercessors to be introduced to the supernatural as He so magnificently had done for me, many times before. So as the team continued to pray, I heard the Lord tell me to look at the east wall in my office and I quickly did. Before my eyes a flame of fire appeared, about three inches long and about an inch wide. Its flame was bright red and orange and it flickered. It was positioned, not on the wall, but right above the wall about five feet from the ground. I was so excited to see it, but also because the Lord heard me! I told everyone God wanted to introduce them to His supernatural dimension. I said, "Turn and look at the east wall." They were amazed to see this flame. It was silent in the room for quite a few minutes, as we all gazed upon God's divine flame.

One of the pastors in the room said to me, "Pastor, you could have put a small pipe in the wall to have us believe it was a divine flame from God." I was so taken aback, to have had one of my pastors believe I would do such a thing, but, even Jesus had many who walked alongside Him and still wouldn't believe. I said, "No, I didn't do this, God did. I asked God to introduce you to His supernatural dimension and He heard me." He continued to deny God would do such a thing, and the flame went out. But, instantly as the flame went out, the same flame appeared two feet higher and two feet to the left on the wall. I said, "Look now, how could I have moved the flame to that position while standing right in front of you?" Eventually the flame did disappear and I turned on the lights. Everyone was in such a high place of faith and began to talk about what they had just experienced. The pastor who doubted me began to inspect the wall and could not find a pipe, a hole, or charring on the wall. He said, "It has to be true, this was God." The Lord told me to tell them this was not like the fire but was the fire which was in the midst of the burning bush Moses saw (Exodus 3:1). It was the same fire formed into a pillar by night in the desert for Moses and the Israelites to follow (Exodus 13:21). The same tongue of fire which was seen on the top of the heads of those who were in the upper room as they were in one accord (Acts 2:1-4). God allowed us to experience that same fire that night!

God wanted to teach me His supernatural dimension, or better said, His supernatural dimensions. He used my office as my school room. He was my instructor, my teacher, and I one of His attentive, and eager students. I learned God was the same then as He is today. What He had His disciples experience was to teach them to go beyond their understanding and mindset. My faith was made greater by God. It was His gift of faith which He increased in me. You see, I didn't know every teaching was preparing me for my future. Every experience I've had in Him was strengthening my faith in Him so my faith would be able to believe in the blind seeing, the lame walking, and even the dead to be raised. Never take for granted God's teaching, precious ones. Learn from your experiences when you are in the valley, or in that place where you stand on the hill top. Every experience you have, is a prerequisite for the entering in, and the development of a greater work which will surely come out of you and from you.

CHAPTER 7

NO WEAPON FORMED

was working for a company in Pico Rivera, California. I was the manager for their data processing center. They were a large company which framed oil paintings and lithographs. It was a distribution center for all types of wall art. When I started this job I noticed I would begin to feel ill every time I went to work. From heart palpitations to headaches, it was as though I was being oppressed, something hovering over me. Other fellow employees were experiencing the same symptoms as I. There was a tension in the air and it affected many meetings which did not end well. Temperaments were high, a strong competitive spirit seemed to own everyone in the office which would not allow anyone to be sincere or even to be trusted. Disagreements and frustration worked hand in hand in our daily lives at work. Something seemed to be controlling this office.

The office was sufficiently well lit by the sunlight through big bay windows and many rows of florescent lighting running through the office, but every office and hallway continued to be dim. What was it? I could feel it, I could see it, and everyone else appeared to not notice this phenomenon. The Bible tells us in Ephesians 6:12, *"For we wrestle not against flesh and blood, but against principalities, against powers, against the rulers of the darkness of this world, against spiritual wickedness in high places."* I would sit in my office and look around and try to see if there was anything abnormal like apparition or demons around me. You may again think I have only one oar in the water, but at that time I was reading about territorial demons and demons who would depress, oppress, and possibly possess. As creepy as it may sound, that was the feeling I would get every time I would come into the office. I would even walk into the warehouse and see if there was a difference in the atmosphere. I would ask myself, "What is it? Is there a curse going through the company?" I allowed my mind to run with thought. I thought of so many scenarios. My mind would go a mile a minute until I would tell myself, "STOP! You're thinking too much and you need to get back to work!" But, every day I would think the same things and know that something was just not right.

I decided I was going to elect myself to come against whatever was coming against the company and its employees. Many were getting sick in the office and others were dying unexpectedly. I was such a young born- again Christian, but so adventurous and always curious of the supernatural. I even challenged the devil one time as he shook my front door and had the door expand and contract, thinking what I saw would frighten me, accept it didn't frighten me, it just made me more aware demons do exist and God is greater and more powerful than he. He knew I wasn't afraid of him; he wouldn't come in my house. I knew then, as I know now, God is with me, who can come against me?

I heard in my spirit there were three territorial demons who were given dominion over this territory. The Bible teaches us in Jude 1:20, *"But you dear friends must continue to build your most holy faith for your own benefit by praying in the Holy Spirit."* Knowing this I ran with it and began speaking in tongues to build my faith in preparation of what I anticipated would come against me. I was going to come against the enemy's cohorts and all he would send my way. I searched the scriptures and prayed God would enlighten my eyes and give me a heart of understanding. I wanted to be thoroughly equipped to fight the good fight. I found scriptures which exhort us to be filled with the Spirit and to pray in tongues which is our God given heavenly language. I found our spirit language enables us to live in the Spirit, walk in the Spirit, be led of the Spirit, have the fruit of the Spirit, manifest the gifts of the Spirit, and go from Glory to Glory until we are transformed into His same image. (Gal. 5:22-25, Rom. 8:14; 1 Cor. 12:7-11,14-15; Eph. 5:18; Acts19:2; 2 Cor. 3:18).

I believe   praying in tongues activates the fruit of the Spirit. It is vital and beneficial to have each of the spiritual attributes become active and mature in us. Praying in tongues helps us fulfill God's predestined purpose for us to be conformed to the image of His Son. (Gal. 5:22-23; 2 Cor. 3:18, 1 Cor. 13:1-13; Rom. 8:29). The Holy Spirit directs our spirit language to pray in accordance with the will of God. The only time we can be assured we are praying 100 percent in the will of God is when we are praying in our spirit language. (Rom. 8:27; 1 John 5:14-15).   When I found all these scriptures I understood I needed to pray in my heavenly language to be in God's perfect will and to activate any gift that would help me in doing so.

The next day at lunch I drove to Smith Park and parked my blue truck in the parking lot, hoping for God to bless me with this gift. I sat and asked God to please give me the gift of tongues. I told Him, "Your Word tells me it is a free gift and I could have it, if I desire it. So I am going to believe in faith that I am getting it and just thank you for it." I started my quest to be baptized in the Holy Spirit with the evidence of speaking in tongues. I read in Acts 1:8, *"But ye shall receive power, after that the Holy Ghost is come upon you: and ye shall be witnesses unto me both in Jerusalem, and in all Judaea, and in Samaria, and unto the uttermost part of the earth."* I knew I was going to need God's power in me. As a novice with a great pining to capture every gift from God, I sat in my truck in faith thanking God for it. I just said, "Thank you, thank you, thank you Lord", until I saw I had only five minutes to return to work. I did this for ten working days straight and nothing happened. On the tenth day I was so disappointed. I asked God, "How could He do this to me?" I wanted Him to be real in my life. I wanted to believe that the Bible, His scriptures were true. I needed this to happen to me. I didn't want any man to lay hands on me and pray for the baptism of the Holy

Spirit! I wanted Him to do it. "Lord please confirm in me how real you are baptize me...please!"

I drove back to work crying like a three-year-old little boy. I didn't care who saw me sobbing and complaining. I entered the entrance of the parking lot of my job. Between my cries I felt a pushing deep within me, pushing past my lips were sounds and words I had never heard. It sounded like a Hebrew language. I was speaking in tongues. I was ecstatic! God is real! His gifts are real! I continued to speak this newly found language and parked and began to walk to the front door to my office. I asked the Lord, "How do I stop this? I can't just go in there and have everyone hear me do this." When I grabbed hold of the door handle of the front door it just stopped. What a relief.

I sat in my office excited, content, and curious. How do I start it up? I went into the bathroom and looked under the stalls to see if anyone was using them before I would try to see how to start up my newly found heavenly language. I faced the mirror and looked at my face in mirror and said, "Okay start...and nothing happened." I closed my eyes and thought of Jesus and was going to pray to Him and to my surprise I began to speak in tongues again, Hallelujah! I had tongues, I was baptized in the Spirit. Yeah! I knew then that God was going to equip me to come against these demons.

I walked into work feeling pretty good. I felt like King David, when he came against the Philistine giant. I didn't have five smooth stones but I had God the Father, God the Son, and God the Holy Spirit. I marched into my office and thought, okay how am I going to do this? I am going to tell all the Christians in the company to pray with me in agreement, these demons will leave and they cannot stay any longer. I will do this tomorrow at lunch time, at exactly 12:00 noon. I went to the warehouse and told about five people who professed they were born-again Christians and three of my co-workers in the office. I had the date and the time for battle.

At the end of my work day I couldn't wait tell Loretta of my mandate and my newly found language. Bedtime was approaching and our boys were getting ready for bed, I told my wife I now speak in tongues and tomorrow I was going to come against the demons. Tonight I am going to intercede to hear God's strategy for winning this battle. She kissed me and told me, "Bring them down, Honey don't let them intimidate you, you're my warrior and I'm sure God's too." Later that night after praying and seeking God's guidance, protection and timing, I was now able and prepared to come against these three demons named Deception, Jealously, and Strife.

In the morning I awoke with an anticipation for battle. I knew my instruction and I knew who I was working for. He is the victor and I knew I would become victorious. I arrived at work and proceeded to implement the strategy I received from God. Noon was approaching and I had to admit I was a bit nervous but I was going to give them the best swing I knew how to hit. I spoke to all my prayer warriors and asked them to begin praying at 12:00 noon. I stood in my office alone and prayed; "Father in the name of Jesus I come against these territorial demons of Deception, Jealousy, and Strife. I commanded them to leave." I declared, "Greater is my God that is within me than He that is in the world! None of you are able to stay because I take back this land, building and company, in Jesus name." Instantly, my office got brighter. People were walking down the hall asking who changed the lights in the office. The office was bright and alive. You could feel a change in the atmosphere. Hallelujah, the giants had gone, and like King David, I hit them between their eyes with the power of God's Word, and they all came tumbling down.

I couldn't wait to get home to tell my wife the mission was accomplished. I had removed those malicious and devious demons. I felt strong and courageous. When I arrived home we greeted each other with a kiss and had dinner. I played with the kids after dinner and finally I couldn't wait to tell my wife about the battle and the victory. After I finished telling her every detail about what God did at my work, she was intrigued and impressed. She said, "That's amazing how you were able to sense those demons and how you weren't afraid to come against them. I am really proud of you." Then she told me she was thankful to God for how He had used me. She hugged and kissed me, again, and I thanked her for her encouragement. Then I asked her, "What about you? How was your day?" She looked at me and said, "It wasn't bad today."

Loretta was employed by a company which serviced dock levelers. She was a one girl office and had five men working alongside her. I have never had a problem with jealously towards this working scenario due to the fact that we both trust each other and she had never given me any reason to believe otherwise. But, this time she said, "It was not bad. I was able to catch up with all my work and ... Do you know who I met today at the office?" "No" I replied, and she said, "The owner's cousin. You know my boss is not really handsome or at all attractive, you remember you met him." I said, "Well of what I can remember, you're right, he's not." She continued to say, "I was introduced to his cousin, and I was shocked because coming from the same family and you know cousins, you would think that he too, was kind of unattractive. But, honey he was very handsome."

I don't know what came over me. Usually my wife and I would describe people we had met and tell each other our opinion of their appearance or how they spoke. Usually I would comment something like, "You're kidding, he doesn't look at all like your boss." I would play a guessing game, as I've done in the past with her by asking her, "Who does he favor Tom Cruise, or Ralph Fiennes? Or maybe Mickey Mouse?" We would laugh and continue our conversation. But not this night. I looked at my wife and said, "Really Loretta? Why would you tell me about him? Are you trying to get me jealous?" She quickly replied, "Of course not, Honey! What's wrong with you? I was only telling you because he is the complete opposite of the two cousins." I continued to argue and ask her if there was anything going on between them. I was so angry with her. She continued to try to calm me down and tell me this was not like me. This escalated to the point I said, "I have had enough for tonight. I am going to bed and read my Bible!"

She found me in bed reading the Bible and I acted as though I was so deep into the word of God I didn't noticed she had walked in. Loretta slipped into bed next to me and began to try to cuddle me and I turned and said, "Please, I am reading right now." She tried again, and placed her leg over mine to initiate a truce of some sort. I turned the page of my Bible and ignored her advances. What was really funny was I didn't know my Bible was upside down and she couldn't bear to tell me. Can you imagine, I was reading my Bible upside down and I didn't even notice it. I was really in a bad state. Loretta finally gave up because I was being stubborn as a mule, and hateful like she had never seen me before. Finally, she moved to the edge of the bed, giving her back to me. "Good night" she said. "Good night" I replied, and placed my upside down reading Bible on the nightstand and turned off the light.

I lay there in the dark sulking, unable to sleep. I tossed and turned and couldn't find a comfortable spot. My wife had moved so close to the mattress edge leaving a big gap between us. I knew she was angry at me and of my behavior. I knew I was not myself but something seemed to be holding me captive and I didn't know how to break away from it. My eyes were wide open and I starring around the room noticed our luggage was standing in front of the mirrored closet doors and the decorative pillows were neatly stacked on the floor, against the wall. I just couldn't sleep, so I laid there and stared towards the ceiling and prayed to the Lord to forgive me of my outrageous behavior. I knew I was awful and wrong but something continued to propagate my behavior. I changed position and turned to my side and was able to see the door to my bedroom, which was on my side of the bed. From under the door a dim light peeked through from the light which was kept on in the bathroom for the children. I noticed something was flowing into my bedroom through the bottom of the door. It was a very dark black oil. It was flowing slowly at first and I began to see it rush in and quickly fill the room. Black oil was invading my bedroom rising up to the edge of our mattress. I slowly turned to my wife and asked her if she saw this black oil which continued to fill our room. She, said boldly "No!" I knew she could not speak due to my obvious character change and in her voice I could hear the hurt I had caused her. "Are you sure you don't see anything like that because I can't even see the luggage or pillows and not even my slippers?" "No" she said, "I don't see anything," and moved even further from me. I became confused because I was viewing such a menacing black oil which had a life of its own. All I could do was stare and pray. "Oh God help me; I don't know what is wrong. I am afraid. Please help me!" Suddenly in the corner of our room an angel appeared. It was at least eight feet tall. I sat up in my bed and raised my right hand towards heaven and thanked God for helping me by sending me this angel.

The hair on my arm stood up like a porcupine. I knew it wasn't an angel of the Lord. I said "Loretta, please I'm sorry. I see a demon and black oil in our room." She took my arm and slid her body close to me and replied, "Yes! I do see the black oil and that big demon, too. Honey I'm afraid." That's when a legion of demons seemed to come out of this false demonic angel, and began to fly all around us. I declared, "In the name of Jesus I cover ourselves with the blood of the Lamb. Greater is He that's within me, than he that is in the world." Instantly, everything left, the black oil and every demon. The atmosphere in our room changed. The anger and tension was replaced with love. It was the love of God we both felt, His agape love for each other. We embraced one another and kissed abandoning ourselves to each other. There was a peace which passed all understanding between us. It was the peace that guards our hearts and our minds in Christ Jesus (Phil. 4:7). We continued to hold each other and fell fast asleep.

What did I learn from this experience? I learned I was not completely prepared to battle these demons. Yes, my God is all powerful but there is a protocol which must be adhered too, when dealing with demons. I remembered the Lord told me, when He visited me, whatever I came against in Jesus name, would try and come against me. I failed to put on the full armor of God. In the book of Ephesians 6:10-18 we read *"Finally, my brethren, be strong in the Lord and in the power of His might. Put on the whole armor of God, that you may be able to stand against the wiles of the devil. For we do not wrestle against flesh and blood but against principalities, against powers, against the rulers of the darkness of this age, against spiritual hosts of wickedness in the heavenly places. Therefore take up the whole armor of God, that you may be able to withstand in the evil day, and have done all, to stand. Stand therefore, having girded your waist with truth, having put on the breastplate of righteousness, and having shod your feet with the preparation of the gospel of peace; above all, taking the shield of faith with which you will be able to quench all the fiery darts of the wicked one. And take the helmet of salvation, and the sword of the Spirit, which is the word of God; praying always with all prayer and supplication in the Spirit, being watchful to this end with all perseverance and supplication for all the saints."*

I was dealing with a demon of jealousy, a demon of deception, and a demon of strife. I suffered backlash and retaliation from those three demons. They were angry with me and wanted to harm me and my marriage. I was oppressed with jealousy which was displayed when my wife told me about the cousin of her boss and jealously overtook me. Secondly, I deceived myself in believing I was in the right, I thought I was reading the Bible but in fact it was upside down. How quickly I was deceived in believing this false demonic angel was sent from God. Thirdly, our quarreling and escalated anger throughout the night was brought on by the demon of strife as I unknowingly allowed him to. How was I so easily attacked by these demons? The Lord reminded me of His word in Revelation 12:11 *"And they overcame him by the blood of the Lamb and by the word of their testimony, and they did not love their lives to the death."* That's it, I didn't apply the blood of the Lamb, from the top of my head down to my feet. I wasn't completely protected. I had put on the armor which we are taught in Ephesians 6:10-18 to do, but I had failed to also apply the blood of the Lamb that day. The Lord continued to teach me my lack of knowledge concerning demonic warfare. In Hosea 4:6 *"My people are destroyed for lack of knowledge because you have rejected knowledge, I will also reject thee, that thou shall be no priest to me.* Although no weapon formed against a deliverance minister can prosper, the enemy nonetheless forms a weapon and takes his best shot. He will use what you came against to come against you. My prayer should have been, "Father, in the name of Jesus I come before you and thank you for who you are in my life. You are my shield, because I put my trust in you. (Proverbs 30:5). I place the full armor of God. (Ephesians 6:10-18). I apply the blood of the Lamb on me and my family. I will not receive any backlash or any retaliation to that which I come against. I pray this in the name of Jesus Christ of Nazareth." I was taught, and I learned, but the hard way!

CHAPTER 8

RIGHT PLACE AND RIGHT TIME

When I came to know Jesus as my Lord and Savior, I was desperate and emotionally fragile. I suffered from depression and panic attacks and needed help. I was born again and blood-bought, but I needed deliverance and inner healing. Many Christians have the mindset when you accept Jesus as your Lord and Savior, from that moment on, you cannot be oppressed, depressed, or even possibly possessed. But I am living proof you can be, and I, without any doubt knew because I became oppressed and depressed. I knew something was wrong with me. I suffered a whole year with anxiety and nerves, and because of that, I became the best actor in town. I learned how to hide my feelings. I was able to laugh when I wanted to cry. I was good at forcing a smile out from a frown. I didn't want anyone to know. I was embarrassed and feared I might have an anxiety attack in front of friends or family, and make a fool of myself.

I know it was hard for my wife to understand or even comprehend her husband's extreme personality change. From a man who enjoyed being with people to not wanting to go anywhere or see anyone. She would tell me I needed to see a doctor or a psychiatrist. I could not deny my condition any longer, something was wrong with me. I made an appointment with the Doctor's office, I knew something had to be done, I couldn't continue my life this way. I sat in with the Doctor and he asked me why I was there. I told him, "I am having bouts of depression and panic attacks." He asked me "Do you know what makes you anxious?" "No," I replied. He asked me many questions about my marriage, children, my parents, and even my job. "I think you just need to slow down and relax. Maybe take long walks and let out all those pent-up feelings which are inside of you." I couldn't see or feel I had a problem with my wife, family, or my job. He said "I am going to prescribe a low dose of valium to take the edge off. Just take one a day, you will feel much better in a day or so." I was ecstatic with my newly found cure. The Doctor finally found my antidote. So I took the pill as directed and waited two days but my condition grew worse and I lost my appetite. I weighed 168 pounds and dropped in a month around 20 pounds. I looked awful, and felt awful, my depression worsened. I called the Doctor and told him the pills are not working. I was worse. He determined that the valium medication was wrong for me. He told me he was sorry for misdiagnosing me and said my illness was not nerves but depression which breeds anxiety. My Doctor replaced the Valium with Xanax which is an anti-depressant. Praise God in a few days I began to feel better and became more active.

To save my job, I used my vacation days combined with my sick days to be able to have a few weeks to recuperate and get back to the life I once had. Many friends and family would tell me it might just be all in my head. I needed to think differently and look at life in a more positive way. I would thank them for their suggestion of remedy but knew that wasn't it. I didn't know what it was, but I knew it was not something I put in my mind. I didn't choose to have long sleepless nights. How did I make myself begin to have fear to leave my own house or have a phobia when too many people were around me?

I would go to work with a Xanax pill in my pocket and a lunch paper bag in my back pocket, just in case I would have a panic attack or hyperventilate. They were my security. It was how I managed to be able to get through the day. I tried to not abuse the pills and learned to only take a half a pill to get through the day to no pill at all. I only took the pill when it became unbearable. My condition was maintained by the occasional pill, my paper bags, and praying to God. Once at work, I began to feel the feeling of desperation.   It always came on suddenly. It seemed to come in waves.

One afternoon it seemed to come like a tsunami, my heart began to beat fast, my palms were perspiring. I was a mess. I quickly walked over and entered my boss's office when he asked, "Al, are you okay? You look as though you have seen a ghost. You're so pale!" I thought, if he only knew, this ghost of mine was trying to kill me. "Please, may I go home? I 'm not feeling well at all." He said, "Absolutely, the way you look maybe you should see a Doctor." "Maybe I will." I replied. I then hurriedly went to my office and grabbed my keys and found my car. I sat in my car and prayed to God and told Him I couldn't take this any longer. I didn't like this feeling. I closed my eyes and placed my hands on my head and wept. I found myself at the lowest state of depression I had experienced to date. I felt broken, of no value, and worthless to everyone as well as to myself. I needed to get home.   My house was my sanctuary; it was my security. I found myself on the freeway headed eastbound on the 105 freeway trying to get home before I would have an attack or something. I gripped the steering wheel so tightly as I kept telling myself ... I'm okay, stay calm! I continued to tell myself to take deep breaths and calm down.

All of a sudden from the pit of my stomach something gripped me and a pain shot through me traveling with a starburst momentum. I immediately pulled over and stopped the car. Am I having a heart attack? I couldn't breathe. My heart was pumping too fast. I felt dizzy, what was I going to do? I saw through the rearview mirror a yellow emergency call box. I knew I had to call someone, I thought. I need to get to the phone. Cars were speeding past me and my car swayed from the sudden wind coming from them.   It was dangerous to even think of getting out of the car let alone walking, but I was dying. I opened the door and stepped out of the car. As I walked towards the call box I noticed my feet began to drag and my fingers and arms began to contort which made it very difficult to walk. It took everything I had in me to get to that call box. I finally reached the phone and with my now deformed hand I opened the phone box and pushed the button. A woman answered and said, "How may I help you?" I said, "Help me. Please help me! I'm having chest pain." While answering her questions my body began to contort even more. My fingers and my face became crooked. The lady who was speaking with me said, "I have sent paramedics with an ambulance to you Sir. You're going to be fine! Don't be afraid they will be there real soon." I said, "Thank you, but please don't leave me, stay on the line with me." She said "Sir, I can barely understand you. I don't know if you understand me right now but you are slurring your words!" I just stood there leaning my body against the call box and closed my eyes.

The paramedics and firemen came and held me and told me to come with them. They carried me and sat me in the ambulance and took my vitals. They told me my pressure was quite elevated. I am sure it was sky high but the word elevated was probably a better way to not startle me more. They took my pulse rate and said, "It is going so fast we are unable to count it. We need to take you in immediately, you could be close to having a heart arrest." I didn't know why but I wasn't able to speak. I tried but words wouldn't come out. I arrived at the emergency room where they asked me for my name and where I lived. I would shake my head because I didn't know. They asked me again what my name was, and my reply was, "I didn't remember." My replies were slurred and slow. I would lie there and cry but didn't know why. They gave me a shot of Demerol and instantly I felt my body relax. They would come in and check me to see my progress and tell me I would be fine. They sent in a nurse to check on me and when she said, "Al what are you doing here?" I remembered that was my name. I looked at her and said, "Kathy, I don't know. I just stopped on the freeway because I couldn't breathe." She said, "You must have had a severe panic attack. Hey Al, don't you remember how you and I were best friends and enjoyed life with all our classmates in college?" "Yes, I do remember." I replied. "This isn't like you

Al, you need to run this off, or swim this off. Just let it out...you understand?" I said, "Yes, I do Kathy." But I really didn't ...let what out? She took my wallet and called my wife and told her where I was. My wife and my parents came and picked me up. They didn't know what to think. The son they knew was outgoing and adventurous and now couldn't even drive home from work. My wife looked at me. Holding my hand she said, "Honey, I can't imagine what you have gone through but I'm sure it has been horrible and scary for you." I said "Sweetheart, you can't even imagine. I wouldn't put this anxiety or depression on anyone. Not even on my worst enemy." She said, "Honey, last night while you were asleep I woke up with fear and anxiety, a desperation I can't describe. I prayed to God to help me have patience for you. I couldn't understand why you couldn't stop it. Now that I have experienced it for myself, I'm so sorry. Mine was just one night and it was dreadful and yours has been for about a year."

Weeks later, I heard there was a Charismatic Catholic Prayer Service at St. Hilary's Church around the corner from my house. I was new to all of this but I was searching to be healed. I walked in the church and sat down about twenty pews from the front. There were two teams praying at the altar. Many people were lining up and asking for prayer. Some were falling down as the hand of one of the prayer team would touch their forehead. Some would cry with joy while others seemed to be so drunk in the Spirit. I sat there and told the Lord, "I hope this is of you. Not I know much, but this looks a little too much for me." I felt a stirring in my body, as if someone was making me get up and walk towards the altar. I found myself in the line to get prayed for and decided it couldn't hurt. I chose this woman on the left of me to pray for me and that's when I heard the Lord's voice tell me not to go to that lady, but the one with blond hair, go to her. I did, and she asked me what my name was and what I needed prayer for. I said, "I need prayer for my anxiety and nervous condition." She told me, "Don't worry my son, God told me there would be a young man who would come with a nervous condition and He was going to heal him." I asked, "Do you think I might be that young man the Lord spoke to you about?" She said, "Yes!" and placed her hand on my forehead and down I went. She didn't push me. I felt as light as a feather falling to the ground. I don't remember anything as I was completely out. When I woke up I felt different. There was a peace in me that passed my understanding, which I later found out it is the peace only God can give you which is described in Philippians 4:6-7, *"Be anxious for nothing, but in everything by prayer and supplication with thanksgiving let your requests be made known to God. And the peace of God, which surpasses all comprehension, will guard your hearts and your minds in Christ Jesus."* I went home a different man. I was free. I was not crazy; I was oppressed with demons. I realized it was better to be at the wrong place at the wrong time, than to be at the right place at the right time and miss God. I know I was at the right place and time. I received my deliverance, my healing, and my peace.

I began to study and pray asking God to enlighten my eyes to understand this depression, and how did I get it. I have learned many times the demon of depression is not the demon who oppresses us first. The demon of rejection can be a root demon, one who enters first. He spreads his claws deep into a person's heart and entrenches himself rooting deep within him. This demon of rejection is a major end-time player for satan's kingdom. It can and does hold hands with self-condemnation, and depression, as well as many others. His main objective is to torment you day and night, while his main goal is to get doors opened inside of you for more of his demons to oppress, depress, or possibly possess you.

What is the reason for being attacked by satan with oppression, depression, and possibly possession? Satan doesn't want you to stay in your God position to come against him and doesn't want God's purpose in you to be fulfilled. Satan knows your purpose, he knows why you were created, he ultimately knows your value. Satan wants this demon of depression to destroy your life, family, career, friendship, and your ministry too!

From a young child with deformity and sickness suffering to breathe to live, to this dreadful depression, made me realize satan wanted me out! He knew my life, God's purpose in me was great. The Lord had me speak audibly, at eight years of age, to the winds. He wanted to have every demon be informed not anything would stop me or hurt me. God's purpose in me and my steps for the world was established.

I have had many visitations with the Lord throughout my life, and one of my first was when I was fourteen years old. He audibly spoke into my ear and said "My son, I have elected you to go throughout the world. Through you I will heal my people. You will be like a Doctor, but you will not go to school for it. My power, I will place within your hands." At thirty-three, I had another visitation with the Lord which lasted for two and a half hours. My floors in my home were covered with billows of white smoke, about two and a half feet deep. I quickly thought it was the wood foundation of my house, that was on fire. The Lord spoke to me saying, "I have waited for such a time as this, my son. I am now going to separate you, consecrate you, and sanctify you, giving you the authority to be under my Glory."

Can you imagine I was with the Lord and He was telling me He elected me? He commissioned me at fourteen but needed to teach me, mold me, and direct me in such a way to prepare me for this day. I was now thirty-three years old. The Lord had been waiting nineteen years for me to be tested and retested until I learned the ways of the Lord to be able to handle His Glory. Through my valleys and hilltop experiences, through my disappointments and discouragements was my learning school. It took nineteen years to graduate to be able to have the authority to walk under God's Glory and no longer His anointing.

I tell you this, because satan knew even as a young child I had purpose in me. God's purpose. He knew I would not only make a difference in the world but be the difference. I was commissioned to go throughout the world and evangelize that Jesus Christ is Lord and Savior. Satan knew my worship to the Lord would bruise the head of every demon. He knew I was sent to help destroy his kingdom. In other words, satan knows you and me. So everywhere I go, I go in the name of Jesus and witches, warlocks, and followers of satan can always sense the God in me.

THE HIGH PRIEST

I once worked at a medical insurance company. I worked with every department and personnel. I loved to work there because I was given the opportunity and permission to have Bible studies in the lunchroom after work for one hour. There were many deliverances and miracles God did through me. It grew quite large and I was happy there were people who came to know Jesus as their Lord and Savior.

One day I needed to take the elevator down to the basement in this two story building. I entered the elevator and a gentlemen dressed in black entered after me. I had seen him before, but I didn't know him. I was positioned a little behind him, and noticed his long blond hair was tied in the back of his head in a bun. I don't know why I just blurted out to him, "How long is your hair?" He turned and smiled at me and said, "Oh about three to four wrist turns. This gives me power, you know?" I looked at him and I felt he was a high priest or warlock, and I said, "I'm not afraid of you, you can't touch me!" He said, "We know." I asked him, "Why did you say we?" He replied "I work with forces of darkness. I, along with legions of demons work together and they know who you are." The elevator doors opened and he stepped out. I continued down to the basement and covered myself with the blood of Jesus as well as putting on the full armor of God and came against any demon who would try to harass me.

I found what I needed in that dark and dank archive and returned to my office. I got busy and continued my meetings and work assignments which I needed to finish before the end of the day. Strangely enough, I forgot about the incident in the elevator with the high priest but evidently he didn't. He waited until the end of the day and asked if he could speak with me. I agreed and instantly covered myself with the blood of the lamb. We found an area in the building away from everyone and he said, "I don't know why but I want to tell you who I am." He looked first straight into my eyes and then looked down at his feet. It was as if he was about to betray someone or tell me something that was to be kept a secret. He said, "Umm my dad is a high priest and my mom is a priestess. They worshipped satan since I was a little boy. He looked at me to see my reaction, but I just nodded. I have been introduced to the dark side since very early on. I was raised in a house with a large basement. This became where I played, ate, and practically lived for many years. I didn't understand why I couldn't play outside with my friends until they told me I was being raised to be the successor of my dad. I had to be separated and trained.

I was trained in curses, and incantations. There were snakes placed in the basement so I would learn not to fear them or not allow fear to overtake me. I saw and was a part of many blood sacrifices, and I can't elaborate too much on that, you must understand. I was given spirit guides and continued to gain power by legions of demons who worked with and for me." I asked him, "Why would you want to tell me this?" He said, "Because in the elevator this morning, it was only you and me. I felt something so different coming off of you. It was like a very strong power, but one I haven't experienced. You see I know about power, satanic power, but yours was stronger. My demons were telling me they know you. They said many times they have tried to harm you and kill you, but your God continues to protect you. Al, I feel your power, I know who you are." I said to him, "Greater is He that is in me, than he that's in the world. When my God is before me, there is no one or anything that can come against me. My Bible tells me no weapon formed against me will prosper." Again, he said "We know." I told him, "You can have

109

this power too! My Lord Jesus loves you, and died on the cross on Calvary for you. In three days Jesus was resurrected. He came back and took the keys of death from satan. Jesus paid the price. You should ask the Lord in your heart, as your Lord and Savior and you will be able to experience His peace, His love, His power. You will be with Him in heaven for eternity."

He looked at me, his eyes filling up with tears. As he walked out of the elevator he looked back at me, smiled and thanked me. A seed was planted, and I know I had faith in God to know this seed planted would one day take root. God wanted that high priest to know there is only one God, the God of Abraham, Isaac, and Jacob. The true King of kings and the only Lord of lords. Hallelujah! How I thanked God in making sure I was at the right place and at the right time to be able to speak to this satanic high priest.

TRANSLATED

Our two dear and close friends invited my wife and I to go with them on a mini vacation. They said the Plaza Hotel has a wonderful pool and great food. They knew we liked fine dining and loved to swim. I said, "Yes, we will go with you." We arrived at the hotel and were given keys to our room, which was located on the ninth floor. My wife was unpacking our luggage and I said I was going to take a few minutes to check out the pool. So I walked to the elevator and when inside noticed there was a sign which read, POOL ON THIRD FLOOR. I pressed the button to stop on the third floor. The doors closed and I stood there anticipating to see clear blue water...yes! The elevator stopped on the seventh floor and a couple walked in and pressed the fourth floor button. He was about thirty years old, his girlfriend around middle twenties. She was bruised all over and her face was swollen, as if she had been in a street fight or something. She wouldn't look up at me but tried to hide her face with her hands. I noticed both her arms were scaly and raw from some skin disease. She tried to comb her hair with her fingers to settle her afro but it was a bit unruly, it would not obey. The gentlemen looked at me and nodded, but wasn't too friendly. I decided to stay in my corner of the elevator and wait. The doors opened on the fourth floor and they walked out. He held her arm tightly in his hand. I was glad they left because he seemed mad at her and the whole world.

The elevator doors closed and the elevator passed the third floor but the third floor button was pressed and lit. I was confused and didn't understand why it didn't stop. The elevator doors opened up on the first floor lobby. I walked out of the elevator and looked around me, still thinking, what had just happened? I walked through the lobby and next to me was same couple. I looked at him, and he too looked at me. He said, "Hey didn't I see you in the elevator?" I said, "Yes." "But we got out on the fourth floor and you didn't." "I know…funny huh?" "Wait a minute" he said, "How can you be next to me when I was on the fourth floor and you were going to the third floor?" I said, "It didn't stop at my floor, it kept on going down." He said, "My girlfriend and I took the stairs but there is no way I could have beat the elevator. I realized God must have transported me. He moved me in time to reach this couple. He asked me "What is going on?" I replied, "God has sent me to you with a message from Him." "You've got to be kidding me," he said. "What's the message?" I told him, "You will not take your life and He does love you."

In front of all the people in the lobby and in front of his girlfriend, he began to weep. He kept shaking his head and covering his face with his hands. He said, "Sir, I don't know you but you're not going to believe what you said was exactly what I needed to hear. Last night I beat my girlfriend almost to death. I had to lock myself in the restroom all night because I was in such a rage. I cried out to God and told Him, "I wanted to take my life and end it all. I told Him you don't love me. Help me, show me you love me!" The way we met up is strange. You couldn't have been near me because we were on two different floors. God does love me...He sent you. I told him I had more to tell him but he needed to meet me on the third floor pool side, in ten minutes.

I waited and prayed hoping this couple would come to the pool so I could continue to minister to them. Ten minutes passed and I was so disappointed. I waited for a few minutes longer hoping they would come. Yes, oh yes! They entered the pool area looking for me. I flagged them down and they sat at the patio table with me. I said to him, "Your grandmother whom, you love and respect, told you not to come here, but you did." He said, "Yes she did tell me but, I wanted to do something I knew wasn't right." I said "Your grandmother warned you. You are a Christian or were when you were a little boy." "Yes, I was Sir". I said "God wants you to come back to Him. Why don't you both ask the Lord back into your hearts as your Lord and Savior?" They both lowered their heads and prayed with me the sinner's prayer. I took her hands and brushed my hands over her scared and scaly arms, in Jesus name. Instantly her arms were clear and without disease, God had healed her. They both wept holding each other asking for forgiveness from each other. They embraced me with all their might, as we three thanked the Lord God Almighty for His cross-pollination, His divine intervention, His love for us all.

Can you believe God transported me through time to be able to be at the right place and at the right time, to be able to walk with this couple. How awesome is our God. Proverbs 19:21 reads *"Many are the plans in a person's heart, but it is the Lords's purpose that prevails."* Can you imagine the Lord used me this way? The Bible tells us about Phillip and the Ethiopian in Acts 8:39-40 *"When they came up out of the water, the Spirit of the Lord suddenly took Phillip away, and the eunuch did not see him again, but went on his way rejoicing. Phillip, however, appeared at Azotus and traveled about, preaching the gospel in all the towns until he reached Caesarea."*

I want to always be available to hear the Lord. To be led by His Spirit to find the perfect place and times to speak into people's lives. Oh Lord, move me, melt me, mold me into whomever you need for me to be. Take me to the ends of the earth to save even one. My purpose is yours. My life is yours. Amen! I pray you too will always be available to hear the Lord. My desire for you is for you to be led by His spirit and have His will be done through you for others.

CHAPTER 9

THE HOLY SPIRIT

God continues to teach us throughout our journey, He is always there for us. He uses our life situations, our circumstances, our valleys, and even our mountain tops, to teach us through them, we have never been alone. He has given to you and I, a helper, the Holy Spirit, who teaches us the deeper things of our Lord Jesus Christ. (1 Corinthians 2:10) The Holy Spirit is the third person in the Trinity. He is fully God. He is eternal, omniscient, omnipresent, has a will, and can speak. He is alive. He is a person. He is not particularly visible in the Bible because His ministry is to bear witness of Jesus (John 15:26).

I wanted to know more about the Holy Spirit. I knew He was one of three, called the Triune God. God the Father, God the Son, and God the Holy Spirit. I continued to research and investigate everything and anything about the Spirit of the Lord. The more I would learn of the Holy Spirit, the more I called on Him. I refer to the Spirit of God as Him, because He is a person not a force or a thing. I have had encounters with the Holy Spirit literally throughout my life. Through every Holy Spirit encounter I am taught, directed, and instructed to be able to know the width, the length, the depth, and height of Jesus. I believe if we knew how the Holy Spirit can help us, we would greet Him first thing in the morning and thank Him in Jesus name for His companionship throughout the day. I have developed a list of what the Holy Spirit helps us with.

The Holy Spirits awaits to do these things for you:

Access to God, Eph. 2:18
Inspires Prayer, Eph. 6:18, Jude 20
Anoints for Service, Luke 4:18
Intercedes, Rom. 8:26
Assures, Rom. 8:15-16, Gal. 4:6
Interprets Scripture, 1 Cor. 2:1, 14, Eph. 1:17
Authors Scripture, 2 Pet. 1:20-21
Leads, Rom. 8:14
Baptizes, John 1:23-34, 1 Cor. 12:13-14
Liberates, Rom. 8:2
Born again believers, John 3:3-6
Molds Character, Gal. 5:22-23
Calls and Commissions, Acts 13:24, 20:28
Produces Fruit, Gal. 5:22-23
Cleanses, 1 Thess. 3:13, 1 Pet. 1:2
Empowers Believers, Luke 24:49
Convicts of Sin, John 16:9, 14
Raises from the Dead, Rom. 8:11
Creates, Gen. 1:2, Job 33:4
Regenerates, Titus 3:5
Empowers, 1 Thess. 1:5
Sanctifies, Rom. 15:16
Fills, Acts 2:4, 4:29-31, 5:18-20
Seals, Eph. 1:13-14, 4:30
Gives Gifts, I Cor. 12:8-11
Strengthens, Eph. 3:16, Acts 1:8, 2:4, I Cor. 2:4
Glorifies Christ, John 16:14
Teaches, John 14:26
Guides inTruth, John 16:13
Testifies of Jesus, John 15:26
Helps our Weakness, Rom. 8:26
Victory over flesh, Rom. 8:2-4, Gal. 4:6
Indwells Believers, Rom. 8:9-14, Gal. 4:6
Worship Helper, Phil. 3:3

We can see after listing all of what the Holy Spirit does, we realize we need the Holy Spirit, to draw us closer to the Lord Jesus Christ. In the Old Testament the Hebrew word Ruach, (pronounced roo'-akh) was used when talking about the Spirit. This word literally means WIND, even the wind associated with a BREATH! In the New Testament the Greek word Pnuema, (pronounced pnyoo'-mah) was used meaning the BREATH or a BREEZE! We can literally think of the Holy Spirit as the *"Breath of God!"* Oh Lord, "Please breathe on me your life, your power, your love."

I want to share with you some of my experiences with the Holy Spirit. My purpose in sharing stories of my encounters with the Holy Spirit is to place hope and create an interest in you to have you seek the Holy Spirit and invite Him into your life to empower you for new supernatural levels and dimensions.

RIDING IN MY CAR

I was driving on the 605 freeway headed north to my workplace. While driving I began to meditate on the Holy Spirit. I thought, could He really be here with me? I mean in my car with me, right now! I thought of the book of Genesis, concerning the Holy Spirit and how He hovered over the deep, that which was without form, awaiting to hear God speak things into existence, and as the Holy Spirit heard God's commands, He, the Holy Spirit, immediately performed it. When God would say "Let there be light", instantly the Holy Spirit performed it, and it was so. I wanted to know the Spirit of God in that way. I asked Jesus Christ of Nazareth to have the Holy Spirit have me speak in my heavenly language (tongues), laying of hands for healing, and whatever I could learn of His supernatural gifts.

That day while driving to work I asked the Holy Spirit, if He was in my car. I was expecting Him to audibly speak to me. I waited and heard not a word. "Well Holy Spirit," I said, "I choose to believe you are with me and you are going to give me a sign you are in this car. Okay, I'm waiting Holy Spirit. Where are you?" I had the strangest idea which popped in my head to say "Marco" so He could say "Polo." I know that was dumb and I began to laugh at myself. A few minutes passed and I started praising God and calling on the Holy Spirit to manifest. Suddenly my right back window began to lower, all by itself. I heard the motor mechanism switch on and as I quickly looked back the window was almost completely down. I said to myself, "You've got to be kidding me!" I pressed the master switch to have the window go up and it went up. Then I switched it down, and it went down. I did this about three times to make sure the motor to control the window was not faulty. I said, "Holy Spirit you were showing me you are in this car with me...Hallelujah!" I realized the Holy Spirit was strategic in giving me a sign. He chose the window which was farthest from me and one I wouldn't be able to reach. Yes, He was with me, and I welcomed Him and asked He be with me for life.

Can you imagine it was the Holy Spirit who divided the Red Sea for the Israelites to cross over? (Exodus 14:21-22). It was the Holy Spirit who brought down the walls of Jericho when they marched around it for seven days (Hebrews 11:30). It's the power of the Holy Spirit who moved mountains and performed by the Word of God. That same power can exist in you. The baptism in the Holy Spirit is an empowering for service which takes place in the life of the Christian (Acts 1:5,8). In it we are immersed in the Spirit's life and power. I told the Holy Spirit, "Alright it's me and you from now on. Let's destroy the kingdom of satan."

IN THE HALLWAY

It was a cold winter night in Pico Rivera, California where my home was located. On that particular night our home was so cold I turned on our heater to warm each room of the house. I had an older home which had a floor-to-wall heater. My three boys, Al Jr. 13, Brandon 10, and Ryan 6 years of age were tucked in bed in their rooms and my wife was waiting for me in bed. On these cold nights, I would do my nightly ritual by standing over the heater, which was located in the hallway opposite the door to our bedroom. I would lean against the wall over the heater to get warm. I would get as warm as I could take and jump into bed to warm us both up.

This night I was doing my "It's too cold and I better get warm for the both of us" and decided to worship God in the process. I looked down the hall and saw billowy white smoke coming slowly towards me. It began to fill the hallway rising about two feet from the floor. I knew it was the manifestation of the Holy Spirit, the Shekinah Glory. The word Shekinah does not appear in the Bible, but the concept clearly does. Jewish rabbis coined this extra-biblical expression, a form of a Hebrew word that literally means "He caused to dwell," signifying it was a divine visitation of the presence or dwelling of the Lord God on this earth. The Shekinah was first evident when the Israelites set out from Succoth in their escape from Egypt. The Holy Spirit appeared in a cloudy pillar in the day and a fiery pillar by night. After leaving Succoth they camped at Etham on the edge of the desert. By day the LORD went ahead of them in a pillar of cloud to guide them on their way and by night in a pillar of fire to give them light, so they could travel by day or night. Neither the pillar of cloud by day nor the pillar of fire by night left its place in front of the people. (Exodus 13:20-22)

In Exodus 33:9 we read, "*And it came pass, as Moses entered into the tabernacle, the cloudy pillar descended, and stood at the door of the tabernacle, and the Lord talked with Moses.*" We see that in verse 9 God is telling us He spoke to Moses from the midst of the cloud. It was His manifestation, His presence which was unfolding before him. The visible manifestation of God's Presence was seen not only by the Israelites but also by the Egyptians: *Now it came to pass, in the morning watch, that the Lord looked down upon the army of the Egyptians through the pillar of fire and cloud, and He troubled the army of the Egyptians. And He took off their chariot wheels, so that they drove then with difficulty; and the Egyptians said "Let us flee from the face of Israel for the Lord fights for them against the Egyptians." (Exodus 14:24-25).* Just the presence of God's Shekinah Glory was enough to convince His enemies He was not someone to be resisted.

As Moses, the Israelites and Egyptians were able to see God's manifestation so was I. I was fascinated in seeing the manifestation of God's Glory and wanted to share it with my family. I called Ryan, my youngest son, to come and see Him, and as he entered the hallway standing next to me he said, "Hey Dad, what is that smoke moving around us?" I knew Ryan didn't really understand supernatural manifestations of God but nonetheless he was fascinated by Him. I told him He was the Shekinah Glory, the presence of the God. I called Al Jr. and Brandon and they too, saw Him. I beckoned my wife to come see and she too, was blessed to see God's Glory. God was showing me it was the same smoke which was seen by the Israelites when they came out of captivity. Scripture tells us they followed a pillar of smoke by day and a pillar of fire by night. Wow! The Lord was having me to see it was the same smoke, the same Holy Spirit manifesting in my house. He was having my faith in Him rise to the top.

After a few minutes the Shekinah Glory lifted and we all went to bed. My wife Loretta and I talked about what God had shown us and how privileged and honored we were to experience such a supernatural move of God. I must have fallen asleep next to my wife and hours later I woke up, because I could feel the underside of my body, from my head to my toes, like the feeling of thousands of angel feathers brushing against my back. I looked around the room and noticed there was a very bright light coming through the window. Its beam perfectly covered our entire bed. The light seemed to be as bright as those Hollywood premiere lights, almost blinding. I noticed the Shekinah Glory cloud was moving through the light and encircling me. He would dance and swoop over me and pass through the light. I was fascinated by the swirling and His movement which I would say, "You have to be kidding me, Wow!" I tried to wake my wife Loretta, so she too would be able to experience Him, but I couldn't move my left leg, as if I had no control over my body. That is when I noticed I was lying down, but suspended about two feet above the bed. The Lord audibly spoke to me and said, "No my son this is between you and me. This is not for your wife at this time." I said, "Is that why I can't move my body?" He said, "Yes." He told me, "I am doing something in you which is supernatural for your destiny and for my purpose. Just enjoy." I laid in that position for a few hours and was entertained by the Holy Spirit's dance.

I opened my eyes and remembered my visitation from last night. I couldn't wait to tell my wife my experience I had with the Lord and with His Spirit. What a night! My wife felt someone staring at her and she opened her eyes quickly and focused. It was me. I leaned close to her face and said under my breath, "Wake up, wake up, I have to tell you something. This is your husband." She must have felt my breath on her or the heat of my body because she opened her eyes! "Loretta, I had another encounter with the Lord!" I described every detail to her and when I finished she said, "Why didn't you wake me up? I would have liked to experience that too." I said, "I tried but I couldn't move my body. The Lord told me it was something He was doing which was between He and I." I told my wife, "Maybe right now I don't completely understand what it all was for, but God knows what He has to do to get me ready for His service."

AMONGST THE MANSIONS

I rented a cabin in Green Valley Lake, located between Lake Arrowhead and Big Bear. Both are world renowned mountain resorts. It is a "hidden gem" in the San Bernardino Mountains. Green Valley Lake's altitude is at 7000 feet, a higher resort community than either Lake Arrowhead or Big Bear. This "best kept secret on the mountain" is secluded, and surrounded by the National Forest. For all these reasons it has remained small, picturesque, and uncrowded. Green Valley Lake has something going on all the time. For a little town, it offers much to do. The lake is stocked often with plentiful fish and has a small beach for swimming.

We filled the trunk with groceries, our luggage, and toys for the boys, and we were off. The drive up the San Bernardino mountains offered such magnificent views of the cities below us. We could see all of Riverside County and the Inland Empire. It was such a clear day which permitted us to see all the way to the ocean. Pine trees, snowcapped mountains, and panoramic views, what more could I ask for. This was a perfect setup for our mini-vacation. I knew I needed to take some time off to catch up on being with my boys and spend quality time with my wife.

We drove up and around the mountain and found the sign that read "Welcome to Green Valley Lake". I was so glad to see that sign, because the boys were getting antsy. During our drive between singing the Wheels on the Bus Goes Round and Round, to playing a game of Who Can Spot Red Cars First, the boys would ask, "Are we there yet?", and of course my reply was always "We're almost there, just around the bend." Then they would comment "But we went around the bend already, Dad." "Oh, I made a mistake, not that bend it's the one ahead of us! They would laugh and sing, "Dad made a mistake! Dad made a mistake!" Thank God that would settle them for a while.

We drove alongside the lake as we entered the town. There were many restaurants and small shops which sold fishing poles and hats and clothing that had Green Valley Lake inscribed on them. It was looking pretty good, we were going to have a great vacation. We stopped to use the facilities and drove up the mountain because the sun was setting and I didn't know how long we would have sunlight.

We saw the most unbelievable cabins. There were large cabins, ranging from two to three thousand square feet. I couldn't wait to see our cabin. I commented to my wife I didn't know my co-worker from whom I rented the cabin had purchased such a large cabin. We drove slowly up and down the street to find the most lavish mountain homes with many chimneys and large glass windows which allowed the beauty of the mountain to be seen from indoors. I couldn't find our cabin so I jokingly pointed to this cute oversized tool shed fashioned in the shape of a cabin which was located between two mansions. My wife laughed and said, "Right Honey that's our little, teeny, cabin. That's funny!" We went up the road and down the road until I said, "Wait a minute I can see a dimly lit address sign on that tool shed. Isn't that so cute?" I looked at the address which was barely lit, and it turned out to be our "mini mountain chalet." That really small tool shed was what we had rented. My wife looked at me and said, "Are we all going to fit in that?" I said, "I don't know. Let's look at the bright side, it could have been smaller!" "What do you mean it could have been smaller, any smaller and the front door would be the back door too, Honey!" she retorted.

We parked and double checked the address and there was no mistake this doll house of a cabin was ours for the weekend. We opened the door and walked into one of the smallest cabins I have ever seen. It was a two-bedroom cabin. Each room measured about 8' x 6' or smaller, which left enough room to fit a full sized bed, and luggage. There was a small one-person kitchen. It was like a hallway with a mini stove, refrigerator and sink in it. The living room was also small, only able to house two wooden chairs and a very small sofa. In trying to make light of our situation I said, "We will all get closer to each other, a close knit family, right?" "Right!
We tried to make the best of it by spending most of our day outdoors. We went swimming, ate most of our meals out, and shopped. We would return to our cabin just to sleep.

One evening after dinner everyone was tired and fell fast asleep. I couldn't sleep for some odd reason and quietly went into the living room and purposely left the lights off. I brought a workbook about the Holy Spirit with me to read. I began to speak to the Holy Spirit and invited Him into the cabin. I said, "Let us have a night together. Introduce me to the more of God." With my hands lifted up, I began to sing "Holy Spirit Thou art Welcome, In This Place." Suddenly, I felt a wave like electricity, a rushing wind go right through me. The Holy Spirit began to dance inside of me, moving downward from my head to my feet. He would turn and move upward inside my body. He was doing this over and over again. To have the Holy Spirit, dancing inside of me was awesome! I continued to worship the Lord while He danced within me. This lasted for over twenty minutes. It reminds me of when the Holy Spirit came in the Upper Room in Acts 2:1-4, *"When the Day of Pentecost had fully come, they were all with one accord in one place. And suddenly there came a sound from heaven, as of a rushing mighty wind, and it filled the whole house where they were sitting. Then there appeared to them divided tongues, as of fire, and one sat upon each of them. And they were all filled with the Holy Spirit and began to speak with other tongues, as the Spirit gave them utterance.*

THE KEYS

The Bible tells us the Holy Spirit will teach us the deeper things. I welcome and appreciate the Holy Spirit. I was once in a very bad situation and began to pray out loud His Word in John 14:26, *"But the Advocate, the Holy Spirit, whom the Father will send in my name, will teach you all things and will remind you of everything I have said to you."* It is important that we know God's word and speak it forth. As we speak His word demons flee and hearing His word inevitably builds our faith. Romans 10:17 reads, *"So then faith cometh by hearing, and hearing by the word of God.*

My wife and I worked for different companies. She always left ten to fifteen minutes before me because her company was a little farther than mine. We both had to be at work at

8:00 am.   On this particular morning we both got ready for work, we had breakfast together and then we kissed goodbye. She got in her car and off she went.   About ten minutes later I reached for my car keys where I always leave them, but they were gone.   I checked my pockets and in all the rooms but couldn't seem to locate them. Panicking I began to search in strange places like in the boy's toy box and the trashcan but I knew the clock was ticking. What was I going to do? I couldn't be late, I had a very important meeting with the owner of the company. I stood in the entrance of our house and prayed to the Lord. "Help me Lord. Let the Holy Spirit teach me and show me the deeper things.   Okay, right now the deeper things for me are my KEYS! Please, Holy Spirit show me where my keys are, in Jesus name." I waited for an answer.

At the same time my wife was on the freeway, headed to work, and audibly heard the Lord speak to her saying, "You have your husband's keys". My wife at the time did not realize the Lord was speaking to her, and thought she was only thinking it and began to argue with herself and said, "No I don't, I have my own car keys." Again, the Lord spoke to her and said, "You have your husband's keys. Look inside your purse!" While driving she searched her purse and pulled out her car keys.   She looked at the ones which were in the ignition and saw they were mine. She realized I must have left mine in the car and when she got in she started the car and payed no attention that hers were still in her purse. She immediately got off at the next exit and hurriedly drove home. As I stood at the entrance of the house asking the Holy Spirit to help me, I heard the honking of a car horn. I opened the door and there my wife was standing next to her car with my keys in her hand, Hallelujah! She said, "Honey were you looking for these?" "Yes I was" I yelled out! "The Lord told me I had them." She explained. I ran towards her and thanked her for coming back and thanked the Lord for the Holy Spirit. Thank you Jesus. We both arrived to work on time and we both don't know how we could have, but again we know a God.

Through my encounters with the Holy Spirit it has brought exciting and powerful testimonies to teach me how to be intimate with God. It is only through the name of Jesus and by the Spirit of God that we can become intimate with our creator. The Holy Spirit wants to be a part of your life. In fact, the coming of the Holy Spirit was equally important as the coming of Jesus Christ! Jesus Christ saves us but the Holy Spirit empowers us to live the life God has created us for. Without the Holy Spirit our lives are stuck in neutral and going nowhere. We desperately need the empowerment of the Spirit to grow and mature in our spiritual walk. The Holy Spirit is our helper to our intimacy with God. The Bible tells us in Jeremiah 29:13 *"You will seek me and find me when you seek me with all your heart."* How are we able to give God all our heart? It is through the Holy Spirit who leads us to God.

The Holy Spirit began to teach me there are five steps to allow us to have a closer relationship with God, which are:

1. Desiring Intimacy with God

To begin your process of finding your deep intimacy with God, you must first look retrospectively inside your heart and calibrate your desire for Him. Are you desperate enough to have your want be more than anything in this world? Are you seeking His heart or have you been seeking for His hand? Those who know the Lord have a sense of desperation for fellowship with Him. He needs to become to you like the air you need to breathe. You need to see Him as your daily bread. Like the word of God reads in Psalm 42:1, *"As the deer pants for streams of water, so my soul pants for you, my God.* In Jeremiah *29:13, "You will seek me and find me when you search for me with all your heart."* My relationship matured to a deep intimacy when the Lord no longer was "**a**"priority in my life, but "**the**"priority.

There have been times in my life when God became my priority because I felt desperate for Him. In these times I had a voracious hunger for His presence—like I couldn't get enough of Him. I look back and see the seasons I pined for Him are still so precious to me, but they were motivated by my feelings. The Lord needs to be the priority never based on my feelings, my emotions, my lack, or my abundance, but only for Him.

2. Being Obedient to God

God wants us to love Him in our obedience to Him. Jesus said this clearly in John 14:15 which reads, *"If you love me obey my commandments."* To have a close relationship with God we see in the above scripture obedience must be allowed to conquer in us, our want for comfortability, our want to do our own thing, and even by rationalizing the inconvenience of God's timing in our life.

If there are areas in your life which you have reserved for yourself, refusing to obey the Lord, your relationship will only wane by your disobedience. 1 Samuel 15:22 says, *"Does the Lord delight in burnt offerings and sacrifices as much as in obeying the Lord? To obey is better than sacrifice, and to heed is better than the fat of rams."* My relationship with God has increased and become more intimate every time I find myself bowing down before the King of kings and allowing Him to reign complete.

3. Loving God Affectionately

In seeking the intimacy of the Lord, the Holy Spirit led me to this scripture in Deuteronomy 6:5, *"Love the Lord your God with all your heart, all your soul and all your strength."* I have learned to abandon myself in worship to Him. I want every part of me to declare, I love God. Love can be cheap and common if your love comes not from your heart. A song of worship sung out of rote proves nothing to God. It is when your love is true you affectionately offer your song from the heart. You cannot give God anything you have not owned first. Being a man I understand many men find it difficult to express their love so openly, but it is the abandonment and boldness of how you express your service, your worship, and your unbridled love for God, which will draw God close to you.

4. Be not Discouraged

Throughout our journey we may pass through seasons of victory or defeat, joy or sadness, or even discouragement replacing the days of encouragement. But, we must take into account God told us in Deuteronomy 31:6, *"Be strong, courageous and firm; fear not nor be in terror before them, for it is the Lord your God Who goes with you; He will not fail you or forsake you."* We are not given the option to give up but to look up. Do not let the enemy deceive you and become discouraged because sometimes we can think God isn't hearing us, helping us, or protecting us, but He is always with us. Remember God tells us, to be confident whatever He started He promised He will complete it. (Philippians 1:6)

5. Promote His work

Jesus modeled this pattern of intimacy with the Father. He regularly sought solitary time to pray, worship and meditate. Out of that fellowship came His Father's work. He knew the Father's mind and felt the Father's heart. That could only be because of His intimate relationship with His Father. We too, are asked to have this type of relationship with God. Through this relationship how could we not want to share of our love of God and His benefits he bestows upon us. Isaiah 61:1-3 reads, *"The Spirit of the sovereign Lord is on me because the Lord has anointed me to proclaim good news to the poor. He has sent me to bind up the brokenhearted, to proclaim freedom for the captives and release from darkness for the prisoners, to proclaim the year of the Lord's favor and the day of vengeance of our God, to comfort all who morn, and provide for those who grieve in Zion—to bestow on them a crown of beauty instead of ashes, the oil of joy instead of morning, and a garment of praise instead of a spirit of despair. They will be called oaks of righteousness a planting of the Lord for the display of His splendor."* As we continue to love the Lord we will find ourselves not able to hide anymore our Love, our God, our King.

CHAPTER 10

WHAT A SONG CAN DO

atan was trying to take away the gift God gave me. Satan tried to remove God's purpose in me. He was trying to take away my weapon of warfare, which was God's worship from my lips. He knew God had anointed me to sing and my heartfelt songs to God would bring an open heaven and begin to heal the sick and raise the dead. You see, I didn't know I would one day travel the world with powerful Miracle Crusades I didn't know I would one day sing to Him, with an anointing which would change the atmosphere in stadiums and in churches all around the world. By singing to Him, the Glory of God would come in with such intensity which people would feel His presence and weep and bow before Him. God had to teach me and reveal to me the ways He wanted me to move in Him through song.

IN THE BEGINNING

I was born in the year of 1952 and at the inception of my life, I contracted a health condition which affected my bronchioles, making it quite difficult to breathe. I was deathly allergic to most foods and many things which were airborne. From six months old to six years old, I suffered with chronic asthma. It would get so bad sometimes I often would have to be rushed to the Los Angeles County USC Medical Center. It would often start with a sniffle, then wheezing, and it would progress to bronchitis, elevate to asthma, and at times pneumonia. It seemed as though I would be at the hospital every week, and at times I would have to stay a day or two to recover or feel good enough to return home. I struggled to breathe every time these allergic reactions flared up in me.

This was my introduction to life for the first six years of my life. I was like a boy living in a plastic bubble. My parents truly had their work cut out for them. They were determined to do everything and anything to keep their son alive because of these intense allergic reactions to so many foods. I had a very low tolerance to pollutants carried in the air, like pollen and dust. They had to cover their sofas and chairs with clear plastic, even the drapery was of a plastic patterned material. Carpets and rugs would not be permitted to dress our floors because it could be a great place to attract dust. I can remember Mom always sweeping, mopping, and waxing our linoleum floors. They would look so shiny and the house was kept like that, at all times.

It was a daily effort to mop, clean, and dust everything to keep my room as well as the house free from dust. Mom realized there would be a great demand placed on her, and a burden to their marriage, but she was determined to keep her son alive. I will always be thankful to this wonderful woman, my mom, for staying up at night, tirelessly consoling me and my dad for unselfishly giving up his time with her for me. It seemed I was always in pain due to all the medications. My lungs struggled to capture as much air as possible to breathe. I remember those days like if it was yesterday, there were days and weeks I would feel well but when the attacks came it was never welcomed. God bless their hearts for I will always be eternally grateful to them. Her drive to help me survive this dreaded sickness began at one of my Doctors visits. She questioned the Doctor of my condition and of its severity. He looked at her with eyes of compassion and could only tell her truth. Mom wanted to know what she was up against. She needed just the truth, nothing more and nothing less but the truth of my condition. "Mrs. Forniss," he said, "I need to tell you what I see. Your son is a very sick child. We have been doing all we can do to help him live a quality life. But what I see is a boy who is going to have many challenges to be able to survive. His tolerance with food and the environment is quite low. If he lives to reach the age of twelve, Mrs. Forniss, it will be a great miracle." She thanked him for his honesty and left the Doctor's office holding me close in her arms.

In the year of 1958 I turned six years old, still having many bouts with asthma. My parents had learned so many things of what I could eat and what would fuel another attack. To give you an example of my severe reactions to foods and the environment; If I ate a piece of a banana, in minutes I would start to wheeze and start sniffling. If I ate one strawberry, almost instantly my lips would swell quite large and my body would begin to react. I wasn't able to walk down the aisle where detergent was kept in the grocery store because I would begin to sneeze and cough and my eyes would swell up. I was not even able to touch or smell the ink of a newspaper because that too proved to be another nemesis.

I can't imagine the pain, the trouble and burden I must have been to my family, due to this dreaded sickness. I often wonder how my parent's marriage stayed strong when my mother's time was eaten up by staying at my bedside day and night. I will always appreciate my mother's sacrifice and I thank God He gave her the patience, the love, and never ending endurance to overcome every obstacle and setback this sickness would bring.

My parents were watching television, and their favorite program ended when a tele-evangelist program came on. Dr. Oral Roberts began speaking and they found him captivating. He was speaking about Jesus Christ, and how He paid the price on the cross at Calvary for every disease known and unknown to man. He proceeded to tell his captive audience, my mom and dad, and I'm sure millions of other people, there is a Jesus healing power, when you pray in the power of agreement, in Jesus name. I'm sure my parents didn't know Dr. Roberts was quoting Matthew 18:19-20 which reads, *"Again, I tell you that if two of you on earth agree about anything you ask for, it will be done for you by my Father in heaven. For where two or three come together in my name there am I with them."* My parents were desperately wanting to find a cure for their son. Dr. Roberts said, "If you have anyone in your home who is sick, please place your hand on him or her and place your other hand on mine, yes, on the television as a point of contact." My dad hurriedly carried me from my bed to their lap and they began to agree in prayer with Dr. Oral Roberts. They both waited a few minutes after they prayed, but saw no changes in their little boy. My dad returned me to my bed, with a sense of sadness and disappointment. Two weeks passed and Mom noticed a slight improvement but had not connected my improvement with their prayer of agreement with Dr. Oral Roberts. They went on with their daily lives still believing it would happen one day.

Two weeks went by and my monthly scheduled Doctor's visit had arrived. They examined me with more tests and x-rays. The Doctor came out after my results to consult with my mom. In an upset voice he said, "Mrs. Forniss, is this a joke?" Taken aback by his question she replied, "What do you mean?" The Doctor sternly said, "Your son...this one. He is not the one we have been taking care of. This son has a normal chest. He is not chicken-breasted any longer. The measurements on his bone structure of his chest is smaller. Even his heart checks out normal, no longer enlarged. Lungs are clear! Mrs. Forniss maybe you are confused, and brought me another son of yours." With assurance my mom said, "I only have one son, (for at that time my younger brother Steven, seven years my junior was not born yet) and that is he." He then said, "Well, Mrs. Forniss whatever you did worked...he is a miracle."

WITH RAISED HANDS

One night, I had a dream given to me by God. It was a dream of instruction. He wanted me to learn worship was powerful. In this dream, I found myself on the top of a tall skyscraper. As I stood on the roof of the building, I could tell this particular building was the tallest of them all because I could see for miles, and all the other buildings paled to this one. There were other buildings rising up from the ground everywhere I looked. I could see cities, states, and nations before me. But I was so fearful, because at that time, I was an acrophobic severely afraid of heights. I mean really bad. I closed my eyes in this dream and my body trembled with fear to the point which paralyzed me.

I heard a voice behind me and I slowly turned and it was Jesus. He told me, "Don't be afraid, my son, I am here with you." I told Him, "I don't like heights my Lord. I am terrified." He said with a most gentle voice, "You're going to be fine, just walk a little forward, trust me." I did and found the courage to inch forward two small steps. The Lord said, "Just a little more." I took a few more steps bringing me closer to the edge and then I stopped and said, "That's it, no more, I can't!" I was getting dizzy and began to breakout in a cold sweat. He said with assurance, "Yes, yes you can, my son, I am with you." He gently placed His right hand on my right shoulder and it felt strong and reassuring. I stepped forward until the tips of my shoes were at the edge of the building. I slowly looked down and saw people who resembled ants and cars which seemed as small as matchbox toy cars. It was overpowering me. I continued to feel a pulling. I kept on saying to myself, "I am safe because Jesus is right behind me and He is holding me." I could feel His precious hand on my shoulder, and that's when He applied pressure pushing me forward and I began to fall. I yelled for all I was worth, "Help me Lord!" I was in such a panic, all I could do was call out to Him.

As I continued to topple over I was just seconds from hitting the ground, when the Lord spoke in my ear. He said, "Son raise your hands to me. Hurry, my son trust me! Raise your hands to me! There is power which will come over you when you worship me, in spirit and in truth. Raise them and see." I quickly raised both of my hands and I immediately stopped in midair. I just stood there standing in the air singing to the King. I looked down at my feet and couldn't believe it. I kept my hands lifted high and began to feel a strength well up inside of me. I felt something propelling me, something surging in me. I began to shoot straight up like a rocket. Higher and higher I went until I landed on top of the building, the one I had just fallen from. I looked at Jesus and said, "Why did you do that, my Lord?" As He pointed at all the buildings, and all the cities, and to all the nations of the world, He said, "I am going to send you all around the world, my son. Just never forget your worship to me is powerful. When you worship me, it will save you, protect you, and heal millions of people." Little did I know my worship to God would one day be used just the way He said, all over the world, with signs and wonders and great miracles manifesting. Psalms 22:3 reads *"But you are holy, O you that inhabit the praises of Israel."* God comes and gathers up His praise. In other words God comes down and is with us. He is in the midst of you and me. His presence brings miracles and heaven opens up.

A SPANISH SONG

I once was asked by a precious young woman in my congregation to pray for her grandfather who was dying in the hospital. He was in a coma for three weeks and his body was already beginning to accept death. When we arrived at the hospital we hurriedly found his room. There he was lying down, very still, with a white sheet that covered him from his neck down. I was so determined to help this precious young woman's grandfather to be healed. I began to pray in Jesus name for God to heal this man. I applied the blood of Jesus from the crown of his head to the soles of his feet. I came against sickness and all diseases which could attribute to this man's demise. Twenty minutes had passed and I saw no significant changes. He was as still as before, and in a coma. Nothing changed. I didn't know what else to do. I closed my eyes to continue to pray, when I heard the Lord audibly speak to me. He asked me, "Are you finished?" Tears began to well up inside my eyes because I was ashamed and embarrassed. What did I do wrong? With such trepidation I responded and said, "Yes Lord, I am. Please forgive me if I came in with false humility or with a wrong spirit. Was I prideful Lord? What am

I doing wrong?" You must understand, when God asks you, "Are you finished?" It isn't a good feeling. All I kept asking God was to forgive me, I'm so sorry.

He told me my heart was right and I did come with the right spirit. He told me, "I don't want to heal him that way." "What way do you mean?" I asked. "Not through prayer," He said. "I don't understand, I'm confused?" He told me, "I have healed a multitude of people and I have done it in many different ways, my son." He reminded me of Naaman who was cured of leprosy by dipping himself in the Jordan River seven times. (2 Kings 5:13). Or when He saw a man who was blind from birth. He spit on the ground and made mud with the saliva and anointed the eyes of the blind man with the mud and he was also healed (John 9:1-12). I said to the Lord, "How do you want to heal this man?" He said, "That's it, you finally got it. You must always find my heart's desire on every person you pray for. Inquire how I want to heal them." "Yes my Lord, I will always wait for your direction. I will always remember to inquire for your guidance in praying for anyone. What would you have me do for this man who is dying?" "My son, I want you to sing to me." "You want me to sing to you, like right now?" "Yes, my son." "Okay but, what song do you want me to sing?" He said, "A Spanish song so that my son who is lying on this table will understand." "I don't know a ny Spanish Christian songs my Lord." "Yes, you do." "No, no, I don't think so." I knew I didn't know a Spanish song, I didn't even speak Spanish at that time, but a few words. He said again, "Yes you do." "I do? Then which one do I know?" "Do you remember the night when you were at Lake Perris and a Spanish church group was singing across the lake?" "Yes, I remember, but I really didn't hear much because it was far away. They were across the lake. I only heard bits and pieces." "It is that song I want you to sing to me." I said, "Well I…" immediately I felt the heat of the Holy Spirit touch my whole body and I knew the song. I closed my eyes and began to sing the song. Can you believe it? I was singing a song I didn't know. I sang it a cappella (without music). God is a good God! I didn't even speak Spanish except for a few words. You know the ones you say to ask for a bathroom (donde puedo encontrar el bano) or ordering your food in a Mexican restaurant (taco, burrito, tortillas). That was more or less my Spanish vocabulary word list. When God calls us, He also equips, enables, provides, and qualifies. This is the song which I sang to the dying man.

"Saturame Senor con tu Espíritu. Saturame Senor con tu Espíritu.
y deja me sentir el fuego de tu amor, a qui en me corazón Senor.
y deja me sentir el fuego de to amor, aquí en me corazón Senor.

Saturate me Lord with your Spirit, Saturate me Lord with your Spirit.
And let me feel the fire of your precious love, down deep in my heart my Lord

.

and let me feel the fire of your precious love, down deep in my heart my Lord

I sang that song for all I was worth. I forgot the situation, I forgot the circumstance. I got lost in my worship to God. I must have sung that song for about five minutes or probably longer, when I felt a hand lightly touch the back of my head. I turned around but there was no one behind me. It had to be an angel, sent by the Lord, to tell me I had accomplished my mission, which was asked of me. I opened my eyes and found myself standing next to the bed of the dying man. But, this time he was sitting up, looking at me weeping and smiling. He was completely healed and released from the hospital. I know a God!

Through this experience God continued to teach me to listen to His still small voice. I needed to always inquire of the Lord in how He would want me to move in Him and to be solely dependent on Him. Let us sing unto the Lord a new song. For our God is great, and He is greatly to be praised. It is a privilege and an honor to have breath to sing. For I will continue to glorify His name through eternity. That is why I was created to sing to the Master. Satan couldn't take away His song, His worship, His praise from me. It wasn't his to take, but only for me to give. It was for me to give to HIM, My God, My Master, and Lord and King.....Hallelujah !

CHAPTER 11

TRIP, STUMBLE, AND FALL

Our steps are ordered of the Lord and are sent with purpose. I have realized if I chose to walk my way and not God's way, I found myself tripping, stumbling, and eventually setting myself up for a fall. Proverbs 16:18-19 reads, *"Pride goes before destruction, and a haughty spirit before a fall. Better it is to be of a humble spirit with the lowly, than to divide the spoil with the proud."* Look at Lucifer who was considered to be the most beautiful angel in heaven, who was created to direct worship in Heaven, and to direct every song of praise to God. Even instruments were placed in him as part of his body to be able to emote perfect worship. He began to allow pride to overtake and overrule him. He began to admire himself rather than looking up to God. He told everyone he too was to be praised and worshipped. Lucifer must have cunningly and persuasively convinced one third of all the angels in heaven to follow him. The betrayal against God banished him and his fallen angels from heaven and removed them from His presence.

Satan doesn't want you, he doesn't care about you! He just doesn't want God to have you. He will do anything in his power to remove you from God, your destiny and your purpose. I know you might be saying you would never let him delay you, distract you, or even derail you. But, many people are caught unaware and they have been influenced by the subtle ways of satan. Satan sends the spirit of pride, self-importance, and a haughtiness to blind you. Even as you are reading this chapter you may not know you have been infected. Let me tell you what pride is. Proverbs 21:4, *"A high look, a proud heart, and the plowing of the wicked, is sin."* What this scripture is describing is a man or woman who carries themselves aloof and believes they are set apart. God tells us we are in sin when we demonstrate ourselves as such. Pride is an abomination to God. Proverbs 16:5 *"Every one that is proud in heart is an abomination to the Lord: though hand join in hand, he shall not be unpunished."* Again, we see God finds pride to be an abomination. What is an abomination? The Webster's Dictionary explains abomination is an atrocity, disgrace, horror, obscenity, outrage, evil, a crime, monstrosity, anathema, and bane. I think we get the gist of how God feels about pride.

We know satan is the father of pride, but how does he begin to contaminate us? Romans 1:22, *"Professing themselves to be wise, they became fools",* —V. 28, *"And even as they did not like to retain God in their knowledge, God gave them over to a reprobate mind, to do those things which are not convenient."* It is when we think we know it all, or when no one's opinion counts and are always right. I am sure you might know someone like that, and quite possibly it could be you. Help us Lord!

CONSIDER IT DONE

I remember once many years ago, I had an usher in my church who was loyal and committed but was hard to teach. We would instruct him on how we wanted something done and he would always reply, "I know how to do this, no problem, consider it done." I had not finished explaining what I wanted nor how I wanted this task to be handled but was stopped because he though he already knew. At the end of the day he would ask us to come and see his work. We would stand and explain to him this is not what we wanted. I thanked him for his efforts but the task was still at hand. He would be hurt when I would tell him he didn't let me finish instructing and he was not easily teachable. You see pride doesn't let you be humble, patient nor teachable. If he only would allow some else's idea to count, double work would not have been created. It may not have looked as though this usher was moving in pride because of his labor of love, but that is exactly how pride is…blinding and deceptive.

THE SINGING COWBOY

Once I was asked to accompany eight pastors to Guanajuato, Mexico to minister in song. I was so excited to be asked and to be used by God. I told them, "Yes, I would love to but there is just one thing that might disqualify me." They asked, "What are you talking about, Brother Al?" I said, "I am not fluent in speaking or singing in Spanish." "What? You don't speak Spanish?" "No, well yes!" "What does that mean?" I explained to them, I can order food like 'tacos' or 'burritos' words like that. There were some phrases I knew, but just a few like, Donde esta el bano? (Where is the bathroom?) and Hola Paco como estas? (Hi Paco, how are you?) These I learned in Spanish 101 in High School. They said to me, "Don't worry your voice is beautiful but more than that it's your anointing which God gave you. Just sing in English and you'll be fine."

A few weeks later I was packed and ready to fly to Mexico. I didn't know what to expect but couldn't wait to see what God had in store. We arrived at the airport and found our luggage. We waited there for our transport. I looked around and saw so many colorful paper flower vendors. I don't know what I was expecting to ride in but a flatbed stake truck came and parked in front of us. We were greeted with a big bear hug by one of the pastor's cousins who sported a jovial smile. We were asked to climb in back of the truck and hold on for dear life. You must remember some of the roads we drove on were dirt and gravel which made our ride very eventful. We arrived at our destination, the home we would be staying in. Everyone was given their bed assignment and I hurriedly found mine. We knew tomorrow was going to be a big day of ministry. They were expecting a multitude of people to join our outside Miracle Service.

In the morning we were treated to a wonderful breakfast which consisted of birria soup (goat soup) and fresh handmade corn tortillas. I was in Heaven! Hundreds of ranch owners and their workers were expected to attend. I could not see a soul but within an hour people began to gather sitting on blankets and makeshift stools. I even saw many little Abuelitas (Grandmothers) walking in the heat of the afternoon aided by walking sticks. Some of the Abuelitas had walked for two to three hours to find a good seat.

It was time to get ready for the service so I quickly showered. I put on my levi jeans and my denim work shirt. My belt had a big shiny buckle and cowboy boots to match. I looked in the mirror and said, "Hey, not looking bad for a city cowboy!" Somehow, I kind of liked the look. The sound system was set up and we were ready to start. I went outside and saw so many hungry people seeking God. No one needed to be asked to worship because right when the guitars began to play, hundreds of voices filled the air. It was amazing and touching. Many shared the pulpit and helped to bring the lost to be found. I heard the host say in Spanish there was a young man from Los Angeles, California who has come to minister in song. As he announced my name I could hear the roar of the crowd which made me feel good. I gave myself a quick inspection of my cowboy apparel and was excited for them to see how I had dressed for the occasion.

Unbeknownst to me, satan had been working on me. I didn't realize I was becoming so prideful. When I heard my name being called and the adulation from the people, I guess I felt as if I was a celebrity. I remember walking towards the pulpit to begin to sing when I noticed I had to jump over this little muddy ditch which had slow moving water. I calculated how to step over this ditch while I waved at the crowd who were cheering me on. I said to myself, "I have arrived! I am going to be a big singing star. Yes, look out world here I come!" Well, being so occupied by my self-adulation and with the roar of the crowd I miscalculated my step to jump over the ditch and I slipped in the mud. I fell face-down in the ditch and my clothes and boots were covered in muddy water. I lay there for what seemed like an eternity but in reality it was only about a minute. A long minute I might add! I said to myself, "Did I just fall? I couldn't believe it!" As I lay there I began to notice this strange odor which seemed to come from the ditch. I realize this odor was cow dung mixed with urine. I was bathed in urine and cow dung, what was I going to do? I stood up and wiped my face and tried to take as much dung from my clothes as quickly as a could while kicking dung off my boots.

With much embarrassment I stood with my head down and heard three men saying something in Spanish, which later I understood. They were hollering they needed to help me and took three buckets of water and all three of them ran up towards me and threw water on my face and clothes. So, now I'm standing with dung, urine, and soaked to the bone. My hair was neatly combed but now completely drenched and it made me look like a middle aged mop head cowboy.

God knew exactly how to humble a man with tremendous pride. They handed me the microphone and I had to sing like that. God spoke to me and said, "This is how I wanted you to be. I can't use you any other way my son until you are humble. There are so many people I want to heal through you my son. But, your pride came in My way." As I sang I wept no longer because of embarrassment but because God had to allow this to teach me how wrong I was. As I began to sing to Him and only to Him, He began to move through me. I was singing a song called "In This Very Room." Many people were receiving their healing and miracles were going through the crowd. The pastors would look at me and some were weeping because of the Glory of God which was being poured upon the multitude. I could hear backs cracking and curved spines being made straight. It was a night I will never forget.

It was now getting later and many had gone but a few remained needing their touch from God. We were escorted into a tent which would fit around fifty people. It was dark because the only light they had in there was a single dim bare light bulb. Many pastors were praying for the remnant of people when I was asked by one of the pastors of the town if I would pray for his son. Because I traveled with my pastor amongst other pastors I knew how not to usurp his authority and asked him if I could oblige the request. My pastor said, "Yes, please go and pray for him!" I got up and walked in the dark towards this little boy of eight as his father held his hand. He told me his son could not breathe through his nose. So I placed my hand over his face and began to pray, "Father in the name of Jesus I ask you heal this young boy of his breathing condition." I was glad he just wanted me to pray for his son's cold or sinus condition, because praying was new to me.

The father took his son and sat down and before I could get off the platform he jumped up and began crying. He said, "Oh my God! God has healed my son!" I thought to myself Sir, it's only a cold! But, he came and took his son by the hand and approached me and said he could breathe, through his nose! So I said, "Amen." He said, "No, you don't understand, my son was born without a nose and now he was given one tonight by God. It's a miracle." I couldn't believe God used me like that. I now know why God allowed me fall on dung that afternoon to humble me to be able to use me for this boy's miracle and others who received theirs.

After the meeting we returned to our rooms. Everyone was amazed and we talked about the day and what God did through us. Some of the pastors came into my room and told me that even though God used me, I was still a liar. I looked at them thinking they were only joking with me but I realized they were not. I told them I was not a liar and asked why would they accuse me as such? They said, "You told us you couldn't speak or let alone sing in Spanish." I said, "I don't." "Then why were you this afternoon singing half the song in English and the other half in Spanish?" I said, "I was?" So they all said, "We heard you!" I was so amazed because it could have only been God to have touched my lips to speak in another language. They told me get ready, for tomorrow you will help us preach in Spanish. I didn't want to because I still couldn't believe that I could. But tomorrow came quickly and we were driven to the plaza where I helped preach in Spanish. Praise God! As I think back, I thank God for delivering me from pride. There were so many God moments that I would have stopped due to my foolish pride. Again, I know a God.

FRUIT OF THE FLESH

Apostle Paul stated, *"Let no one think of himself more highly than he ought."* (Romans 12:3) When you think of yourself more highly than you are you are setting yourself up to become blind. In Galatians 6:3, *"For if a man think himself to be something when he is nothing he deceiveth himself."* When you think of ourself more than what you are an open door of pride will always take you over. I have listed a few men in history who have been blinded by pride which ultimately became their fall.

Adolf Hitler - He was a man who was constantly raving about conquering Great Britain, envisioning a thousand year Nazi dynasty. He was completely taken over by pride and power. Where did he end up? Dead by his own hand in a bunker in a ruined Germany.

Napoleon Bonaparte - This prideful Emperor of France crushed every foe under his feet. Upon entering Milan, Italy, Napoleon summoned the archbishop of the church and demanded, "Prove to me there is a God and the Bible is the Word of God." The archbishop never uttered a word but simply pointed to Napoleon's leading soldier, General Mesina, a Jew. Prideful as he was, the Emperor recognized the truth of what the archbishop had revealed, shouted a command, turned his horse around and together with his troops galloped away, without firing a shot! If there is no God there would be no Jew, for Abraham was a hundred years of age and Sarah ninety when Isaac was born. Where did he end up? In exile and disgraced on the Island of St. Helena! Before he died, however, he confessed his faith in Jesus Christ as the son of God, to his trusted friend General Bertrand.

Voltaire - This man was an atheist full of pride, who almost destroyed France with his twisted philosophies. He was going to rid that nation of every Bible and dethrone God. He boasted within one hundred years there wouldn't be one Bible left in France, except in some dusty old museum. He was the epitome of a complete prideful man. Before his death, Voltaire became demented and the nurse attending him declared for all the money in France she would never again nurse another dying infidel. When the Doctor, nurse or friends entered his room he would shrink back in his bed and shriek, "the Nazarene, the Nazarene!" Just before his death Voltaire screamed, "Thou has conquered, Thou Nazarene." Ironically, the very house in which Voltaire lived was purchased a hundred years later, and turned into a Bible Publishing House.

Satan is not a respecter of persons, his method of operation is to steal, kill, and destroy and he uses pride which he sends to oppress us. Pride steals the real you, kills your God opportunities, and destroys relationships within your circle of influence.

Exodus 14:14 reads God fights our battles against satan. What does it mean when God tells us He fights our battles? It means we do not have to have anguish, be anxious, or be discouraged when we are being attacked. When it seems a situation is hopeless or the matter at hand is too overwhelming, we may be tempted to doubt God. But Christians must remember no problem is beyond the scope of God's sovereign care for His children. He has promised to take care of us (Philippians 4:19), make good plans for us (Jeremiah 29:11), and love us beyond measure (Romans 8:37-39). He doesn't want to lose anyone.

The Lord tells us the Fruit of the Spirit is; love, joy, peace, patience, kindness, goodness, faithfulness, gentleness and self-control which He asked for us to have in us. Satan mocks God by giving God's children a counterfeit with the Fruit of the flesh which is the complete opposite of what the Fruit of the Spirit is. The fruit of the flesh is; hate, sadness, disharmony, impatience, unkindness, evil, disloyalty, hardness, and unrestraint. I pray to God we will allow Him to have us recognize if we have been moving in any of these. I mentioned the fruit of the flesh because the spirit of pride breeds them their existence in us.

A Dirty Pool

We were asked to join our dearest friend and her three teenage daughters to stay for the weekend in a Palm Springs resort. We thanked her for the invitation and quickly said, "Yes we would love to." It was about two weeks away and we began to prepare for our weekend oasis getaway. My wife packed her luggage with all the things she would need for those two days. She packed her make-up, cream, suntan lotion, perfume, shorts, blouses, sandals and her swim wear. She told me, "Honey, you better start packing because you don't want to pack at the last minute." I told her, "I'll get right to it!" I walked upstairs and began to pack. While packing I told my wife I needed a new pair of trunks. She said, "But you have so many already." "I know", I replied. "But we're going to Palm Springs and I want to sport a nice bathing suit". I began to walk around the room as if I were modeling trunks down the runway. We both laughed and I said, "I know I have quite a few but one more won't hurt, right?"

That afternoon I took a trip to Macy's and couldn't find a pair to fit. I shopped the whole day and I couldn't find the pair which I envisioned as I walked around the bedroom modeling my imaginary perfect trunks. By the end of the day the sun was setting and I passed a Big Lots Store. It was not a very high-end store but I thought maybe they might have what I'm looking for. I walked in and began to look in this huge bin which held bathing suits in all sizes and colors. I found some which were not bad but yet not what I was looking for. At the bottom of the bin I saw black trunks which had my name on them. The material was jet black in color and was my size. They were a perfect fit and I wanted them. I knew they would look good on.

I returned home and showed my wife my new trunks. "I'm going to look so nice in these trunks." She told me, "Honey, don't you think you're being a little prideful? I mean you took all day to find those trunks. Don't get me wrong but you're going to be in the water and no one is going to see if they are baggy, nice, expensive or cheap." "You're probably right," I replied. But inside my mind I was thinking, "But, I'm glad I bought them anyway."

God knows how to battle for you. He knows what He needs to do to humble you back to Him and that is what He did to me. He flat out, without question humbled the pride out of me! We arrived at our condo inside the resort and unpacked. Lunch was served and we ate. I couldn't wait to go to the pool. I commented, "Hey, is anyone wanting to go swimming?" And everyone said, "Yes!" We quickly cleaned up the kitchen and put on our bathing suits and I looked in the full length mirror and said, "I really like these trunks. They are my favorite pair." I walked downstairs and our friend commented on them and said, "Those trunks are nice on you, Al." I said, "Oh these trunks? Oh thank you!" My wife said, "Oh yes those old trunks and laughed." She passed me and said, "Don't forget pride comes before destruction."

We walked down a path which led to their beautiful pristine pool and we placed our towels on lounge chairs reserving our spot. There was no one else in the pool except for my wife, our friend, and her three girls. The day was hot and the pool was inviting. I was the first to dive in. I came up from my dive and began to swim across the pool. What a wonderful time we were having. The girls were gathered together and I was busy swimming back and forth, end to end, when I noticed the pool was not so clean. I could see the pool was not as clean as I thought. There was hair all over the bottom of the pool. It was so gross I was debating whether or not to get out of the pool. The others commented it wasn't like that before. "What could have happened?" I said, "I don't know but I'm getting out." They were all right behind me as I began to step out of the pool when I noticed all those strings which were at the bottom of the pool used to be my swim trunks. All that was left of my trunks was the elastic waistband and the very transparent netting. My trunks were in shreds and I was almost completely naked. I ran out of the pool, took my towel and hurriedly wrapped it to cover my nakedness. They were laughing and crying at the same time. My wife yelled out to me saying "I told you pride comes before destruction!" I stood there with egg in my face, or should I say trunkless.

God saw I was being prideful. I didn't see it at first. Pride always deceives and blinds you. I thank the Lord for doing what He needed to do to get my attention and my attention, did He get. It wasn't the fact I couldn't find a nice pair of trunks, or I took time to shop for them. It was my attitude, my haughtiness, my self-importance. This happened early on in my Christian walk.

Sometimes we think our test for change is over and we have learned our lesson. Well, there has been many testings which have melted me, molded me and realigned me to remove what doesn't belong in me. When the Lord recognizes pride wants to come in again, He always reminds us in one way or another for us to be cognizant of what spirit you are entertaining.

THE BROKEN CHAIR

This reminds me of the time I had written a play, produced it and directed it. It was given to me from God while I was in a cabin alone in Big Bear Mountain Resort. I prayed to God that night to use me in whatever He wanted to do through me because I was ready. I waited for a while and continued to pray for about an hour. Suddenly He told me to get a pen and paper because He wanted to develop a play which He wanted me to introduce to the church. While I ran to find a pen and some paper He began to speak. Within thirty-five minutes He had given me the story line, each role, their lines, the sets, and wardrobe. It was quick and precise. I wrote everything down on an old calendar which I found in the kitchen. Can you imagine, God loves to create plays too. Amazing! I knew I had something between the pages of the calendar because everyone who I would tell the story to would laugh, and then cry. They would tell me this play was so professional.

I made sure to do precisely everything the Lord had given me that night in the cabin. From the sets to the wardrobe it was perfect. On opening night, the church was packed. The play started and I was nervous. Please I prayed let everything go right. Let the actors not forget their lines or miss their cues. I observed the audience so attentive. They were glued to their seats in anticipation. I would see them emotions take a turn from weeping to laughing. The play was such a success.

After the play many came to me and gave me compliments. My head began to swell with pride with every compliment which was given me. Receiving such acknowledgments are truly heartwarming and brings a feeling of accomplishment. There is a fine line between being proud of what God has or is doing through you compared to receiving accolades and allowing it to pass proudness becoming pride which deceives you all together. I would tell them, "Thank you so much, praise God!" But I liked the feeling of being accomplished and successful. Something was happening to me. I was forgetting this play was not mine at all. All creativity was God's. He instructed me in what to do, how to do, and when to do them. It was not my play it was His. I just crossed over that line and knew correction, instruction, and a fall would surely be directed my way. Oh my Lord!

My experience with the Lord in creating this play reminds me of when Moses built God's tabernacle. God gave Moses the measurements, the colors, and the exact materials to use. God designed it, not Moses. God said to Moses in Exodus 25:9, *"Make this tabernacle and all its furnishings exactly like the pattern I will show you."* That is exactly what the Lord did with me. It wasn't my play at all, it was God's. The song I sing, "My Tribute" is the epitome of how we should be at all times. The song goes like this:

How can I say thanks for the things you have done for me. Things so undeserved yet you gave to prove your love for me.   The voices of a million angels could not express my gratitude. All that I am and ever hope to be, I owe it all to thee.

To God be the Glory.   (Then it continues)

Just let me live my life and let it be pleasing to thee, And if I should gain any praise, let it go to Calvary.

The next day at church the senior pastor was sharing with the congregation on how well the play went. He began to speak about me and how great a talent I had. Many were looking at me and clapping. I would nod my head and smile. Deep inside of me I was taking in all the praise and accepting all the credit. Again, I didn't see it. Pride was slowly forming but surely infecting me. I was seated in the middle of the sanctuary with my wife and children and stood up and thanked everyone. I intently   listened to our pastor's sermon thinking how great and loving our God is to have giving us His word. During the middle of his sermon everyone heard the loudest bang, and all were looking around to find the source. My wife looked at me and then for me.   My chair had broken into pieces and I sat flat on the floor. The congregation found the source of the bang and it was me. They began laughing with some pointing their fingers towards me. I couldn't blame them for reacting that way because it was awfully funny but at my expense, my humiliation. I again was reminded of how much

God loved me to teach me I had crossed over and this retribution I so welcomed. I didn't know what to do. But, God did. God had to put me in check once again. He wasn't happy with me and I knew it. An usher picked up the broken chair and replaced it with another one. I sat and asked God to forgive me. This happened early in my relationship with Jesus.

You see pride sneaks in quietly and tries to overtake you. Thank you Lord for the times you had to help me see my faults and how much you loved me to correct them. Hallelujah, I know a God!

CHAPTER 12

GOD THAT PROVIDES

One of my very favorite names of God and one through the years has meant the most to me is **Jehovah-Jireh "The Lord will provide"**. God revealed Himself as the Lord who would provide way back in the first book of the Bible, Genesis. Abraham was ready to sacrifice his son Isaac on an altar at the top of a desolate mountain in the land of Moriah. We know it was desolate because when they reached the base of the mountain, Abraham took with him the wood, fire, and knife which would be needed to complete the sacrifice. He must have known none of those things would be found at the top. He also took Isaac who was to be the sacrifice and left two servants behind. Abraham said, "We will return", denoting he knew God would provide.

Nearing the top, Isaac said, "Behold, the fire and the wood, but where is the lamb for the burnt offering?" Abraham said, "God will provide for Himself the lamb for the burnt offering my son." Just as Abraham was about to kill his son, the Lord stopped him and showed him a ram caught in a thicket and told him to use it instead. God had placed the ram nearby in advance, knowing He was going to need a substitute for Isaac. After the sacrifice was complete, Abraham named the place "The Lord Will Provide" which in Hebrew is YHWH-Jireh. "YHWH means Jehovah" and "Jireh" translates into "Provide" which is a word with wonderful Latin roots. Pro means "before" and video means "to see". So, it means to see in advance or before the need is known. God is preparing an answer before we know there is a need. Genesis 22:1-14.

I have seen throughout my journey God continues to teach me to trust Him with my finances. It wasn't easy to trust Him with what little we had. One thing my wife and I never failed in doing was to give our tithes to God. In Luke 6:38, *"Give, and it shall be given unto you; good measure, pressed down, and shaken together, and running over, shall men give unto your bosom. For with the same measure you measure it will be measured back to you."* I knew this meant I needed to put God first in my life and that included tithes and offerings. In Malachi 3:10 God challenges us to prove Him with our monies. God wants to break open the floodgates of heaven and shower upon us a blessing which is so abundant which we shall be overwhelmed by it. God is longing to send a tsunami of spiritual blessings to us. What is holding it back from us? We have the key God places in our hand but are we unlocking the door of our blessings? What unlocks the door for us are the keys of faith in our commitment to God in tithes and offering. One must understand God is not wanting your monies because He owns all the silver and gold and the cattle of a thousand hills, in other words He owns all. Tithes and offerings are a principle of faith more than a principle of finances. When Jesus hung on the cross He paid the price for everything fulfilling the law. We today are not commanded to give but our love for Him should command it. 2 Corinthians 9:6-8 reads, *"But this I say, He which soweth sparingly shall reap also sparingly; and he which soweth bountifully shall reap also bountifully. Every man according as he purposeth in his heart so let him give; not grudgingly, or of necessity: for God loveth a cheerful giver. And God is able to make all grace abound toward you; that ye, always having all sufficiency in all things, may abound to every good work:* If we don't give it will not be given. The Bible tells us we must first give to the Lord our tithes and offerings and He will bless us. We only move God's heart by our want to give Him than by us feeling we have to. How can our God not want to pour out provision, protection, and health etcetera when He finds someone who displays total trust in Him.

Many times people have asked me to pray for their finances and I have. The Lord told me I was out of order and I was not adhering to scripture. He told me I could not pray for someone who has not given their tithes and offerings to Him. He directed me to Luke 6:38 which tells us we must give before we can receive. You see those who don't tithe curse themselves. They must adhere to the word of God and be in position to be blessed. Again, God wants to see if you love Him enough to have faith in Him to give. There is not any prayer to bless your finances other than to pray you receive revelation on the algorithm of financial blessings.

Below are some of my most significant testimonies where God became Jehovah-Jireh the "Lord will provide." I pray they will encourage you to change your mind set on giving.

THE SECRET OF SELLING

God told us to sell our home which we lived in for twenty-two years. I wasn't happy to hear that because our home was refurbished and remodeled twice within those years. We were pleased to see our home transformed into our dream house which was picture perfect. The Lord continued to tell me I was to sell the house. So, I told my wife I needed to tell her something which might be quite disturbing. She said, "What is it?" I said. "God told me we are supposed to sell our house. I know it seems crazy because we just finished all we wanted to do to our home." I anticipated my wife to be upset and tell me, "No way, Honey that's not happening." But, she looked at me said, "Yes, I know because God has been telling me the same thing." On one hand I was relieved she agreed with me but on the other hand I was saddened because I loved our home.

We found a realtor and put the house on the market. Our house was one of the most updated homes in the block, it had great curb appeal. Weeks had gone by and many people came to view the house but no offers were given. I couldn't understand it. The house had a remodeled kitchen with oak cabinets, a sunken den which wrapped around a beautiful pool, a floor-to-ceiling brick fireplace in the den, and my bathrooms were remodeled and extended. There were homes which were selling down the street for almost the same price but were not even close to the quality of our home. I couldn't understand why.

After about a month we were going to take it off the market when the Lord spoke to me. He said, "How do you expect me to help you sell your house. I gave you this house and I can't take it back to bless someone else with it until you release your house back to me." I told the Lord I didn't know I was supposed to do that. I thanked Him for helping me understand how everything touches the supernatural. I asked my wife to pray with me in thanking and releasing our home back to the Lord. I said, "Father in the name of Jesus I thank you for this house you gave me. It has been a blessing for me and my family. I appreciate the years we have been able to live here. I now need to sell it so I release this house back to you. Please find the right family who will be blessed to have this home. We pray this in the name of Jesus. Amen!"

In the morning we received a call from the realtor giving us the good news. He said. "You have a strong offer. They are giving you the asking price but with a condition." I said, "And what would that be?" He replied, "You only have a month to move because they want to be in the house before Christmas." Can you imagine? No matter what we did we couldn't sell the property until God told us to release it back to Him and when we did, it sold the next day. That was fast and so God!

We began packing and sorting what we were going to take and what we were going to either give or sell. I suggested to my wife we should hold a yard sale and sell what we were not going to need. She agreed it was a great idea. I began carrying things out to the front yard when the Lord spoke to me and asked for me to make a sign for the sale. I found a white piece of cardboard and started writing For Sale.

I finished the letter F when the Lord audibly told me He would spell it for me. I wanted to tell Him I didn't need help to spell, but He said, "Please let me." Alright! I already had F written down and then He said, "O and then R." I was just about to write down an S when He told me I was misspelling the word. He said to me, "Write down the letter F." "You want me to write down F?" I questioned. "I need an S not an F, Lord." Then I clearly heard Him say the letters R,E,E. "You have to be kidding me Lord, you want me to give away the things that I am selling?" "No, my son, not the things you are selling, I want you to get all your furniture, everything that's in your house other than your beds to sleep on and your clothes!" I had new and re-upholstered sofas and chairs. I had high-end furniture and pictures. "Everything Lord? I asked." "Everything." He replied. When I told my wife what the Lord had said it bore witness to her spirit and she said, "Absolutely!" We took everything outside and placed the sign out so everyone would see it. We left for about an hour and when we returned home everything was gone. I am quite sure the neighbors were happy with our mandate from God.

I told my wife it would be hard to find a house so quickly and maybe we should convert one of the offices of our church to stay in for a while. She agreed and asked me how long did I think it would take to find our home. I said, "Oh, maybe about one-to-three months not much more." She replied, "I can do that but not much past that. You promise right?" "Absolutely!"

We took our beds and clothes and some personal items and converted two church classrooms into our temporary bedrooms. My boys were teenagers and they were a bit uncomfortable with this whole situation. I understood their discomfort because they have always had their own rooms and their privacy, but they made the best of it. The three months had come and gone. My wife came to me and asked, "Well, when are we leaving to find our own place?" I would tell her I didn't know. I told her I was sorry but God had not released me as yet. From believing to only live there for three months, turned into almost five years. One night my wife became very angry and told me she was tired of living without having her own home. She told me we didn't even have monies for Christmas presents. She was upset with me as well as with God. She said, "How can we be serving God and be in this situation?" She marched to our bedroom crying and asking God why? I knew she was on her last straw when I heard our bedroom door slam shut.

I stood in my office and began to pray. I too, was confused! I didn't expect to stay as long as we had. I did ask God what did I have to learn from this ordeal? He was silent. I heard not a word from Him. I went down to the sanctuary when I heard my Worship Director rehearsing. I walked in and greeted him and asked how he was. I had to use all my strength to muster up a smile to hide the fact I was so unhappy, fed-up, and discouraged. I looked at him and said, "You know what?" He said, "What?" "You are a somebody, right?" He replied, "Yes." "Well, give me both your hands because God tells me to find somebody to agree with on anything in Jesus name and I could consider it done. Come on give me your hands so we can pray, I need something done quickly!"

We stood in the middle of the sanctuary and I prayed God would place money in my hand by tomorrow morning so my wife would not be so discouraged and we could buy Christmas presents for our grandchild and family. After my prayer I said, "In the name of Jesus of Nazareth I believe!" My Worship Director smiled at me and said, "You mean business Pastor, Wow!" After rehearsal I went upstairs and very quietly opened our bedroom door and slipped into bed and fell asleep.

I was awakened early in the morning by a phone call. An elderly brother of the Lord who was not a member of my church, I might add, said, "Pastor, how are you? I was jogging this morning and the Lord audibly spoke to me!" "He did?" I replied. "Yes, and He told me I was to bless you today." "He did?" "Yes! He told me go now and bless my son, so that is why I called you." "Amen" I told him. "Are you free this morning? Can I meet you at the church?" "Yes, we can meet. He asked, "What time?" I said, "Well, I am at the church right now." "Then I will be there in ten minutes."

I got out of bed, put a baseball hat on to hide my uncombed hair, jumped into running shorts and tee-shirt. I didn't even brush my teeth. I ran down the hall and stood in front of the door to hear the ringing of the doorbell. I was ready. I was excited, I know a God who heard my petition. I was ready to receive my blessing. A few minutes passed and the doorbell rang. I so wanted to open the door immediately but I knew it would be obvious I was standing there waiting, so I counted to ten and slowly opened the door. "Good morning man of God!" I said. He hugged me and said, "Blessings to you Pastor Al. I must run but I want to give you this." and handed me a check which was folded in half. I placed it in my pocket and thanked him. We hugged and he left. As I closed the door I was jumping around and singing Hallelujah! Thank you Lord. You don't know how much I had to control myself because I wanted to see how much the check was made out for but I knew if I viewed it in front of him, it would be rather rude. I got the check out and saw it was for $1,000.00. Praise God!

I ran upstairs and opened our bedroom door and said to my wife. "Honey, I know a God. He cares about us. He sent this precious brother to give us a $1,000.00. See, God is our provider!" We both cried and hugged each other. We thanked God for His faithfulness and asked that He forgive us. We also forgave each other for things we said to each other. I told my wife we must pay our car payment but let us also take two families and buy their children their Christmas clothes and presents. God stretched our monies to be able to do that and buy our family their gifts too! We had a great Christmas.

Years had passed and my wife unbeknownst to me had woken up in the middle of the night and cried out to the Lord concerning her wanting to have her own home and privacy. She got out of bed and walked downstairs to our sanctuary and laid face down on the altar. She told God if the church was going to be her home she was now okay with it. She told God the church's nine classrooms were like her nine bedrooms, the sanctuary was like her living room which now can accommodates two-hundred people, she now had six bathrooms, two stairwells, our fellowship hall was now her dining room which now seats one hundred guests, and thank you for her very large kitchen. She felt her body be filled with peace. She got up from the alter and said, "God it is well with my soul."

Two weeks later God spoke to me and told me to go find a house. I found a house I could not afford nor qualify for. It was a mini-mansion in a gated community overlooking a lake and a golf course. It was a five bedroom, five bath home with maid's quarters. This home had everything you could think of. We had an outside kitchen, pool, waterfall, gazebo, and much more. We walked into this house and spoke to the owner. After speaking with her for a few minutes God gave me a prophetic word to give to her. I spoke of her son, his business and into her life. She began to cry and tell me she wanted us to be in her home. Three days later we had the key to this $1,600,000.00 mini-mansion. Not only did we have divine favor with the owner but a prophet of God called me around the same time and told me someone was going to give me money to furnish a new home. A few days later another prophet said God asked her to give me $70,000.00. Can you imagine God showing and instructing two prophets; one to give the money and the other to instruct me what to do with it?

God told me the five years duration in the church could have been for only a few weeks to a few months. It was a test for my wife. God wanted my wife to let go of all and allow Him to reign in all of her life. He wanted her to tell Him it was well with her soul, to trust Him in whatever He wanted to do with her, and she would be content. The minute she told Him, "Yes Lord it is well with my soul."......He began releasing our blessings.

This reminds me of the story of Job. In the book of Job we read satan appeared before God in heaven. God boasts to satan about Job's goodness, but satan argues Job is only good because God has blessed him abundantly. Satan challenges God, if given permission to punish the man, Job will turn and curse God. God allowed satan to torment Job in order to make this bold claim, but he forbade satan to take Job's life in the process. In the course of one day, Job received four messages, each bearing news his livestock, servants, and ten children have all died due to marauding invaders or natural catastrophes. Job tears his clothes and shaves his head in mourning, but he still blesses God in his prayers. Satan appears in heaven again, and God grants him another chance to test Job. This time, Job is afflicted with horrible skin sores. His wife encouraged him to curse God and to give up and die, but Job refuses, struggling to accept his circumstances.

Three of Job's friends, Eliphaz, Bildad, And Zophar, come to visit him, sitting with Job in silence for seven days out of respect for his mourning. On the seventh day, Job speaks, beginning a conversation in which each of the three men share their thoughts on Job's afflictions. He, after hearing all three begins to tell them their wisdom is not valid. He does want to ask God how could He do this to him, but cannot find it in himself to do so. He says the redeemer will vouch for his innocence. He is blameless. He began to complain and murmur but realized God is God. He told God he knew God knows all things and nothing was impossible with Him. Eventually God blessed Job with twice as much as he had before.

My wife Loretta had gone through a Job experience and realized God had to be God in her life. She went to Him and told Him, "I am yours my Lord and you are mine. My life, my family, my husband, my home, my heart is yours. It is well with my soul." Just like Job, my wife surrendered all. Throughout our walk the Lord has continued to show us He is

God, God of our finance and Jehovah-Jireh, our God that provides. Some people might think our blessings are only monetary, but that isn't true. He blesses us in many different ways. If we are faithful to Him, in prayer, in tithing and in our worship to Him, He is forever faithful to us.

THE MIRACLE BOY

My son Ryan was around sixteen years of age when he came home from school one day and told his mom he was not feeling well. He asked us to pray for him and we did. Afterwards he went to lie down and slept, missing dinner. In the morning he went to school but again came home and complained he had a nauseous stomach. My wife felt he was coming down with a stomach flu and gave him medicine to quiet his stomach. She continued to question how he was feeling and if he was suffering with other symptoms. He would just say, "No." This went on for about a week and a half and he was looking pale and very lethargic.

My wife called my mother on the phone to tell her about Ryan's condition and my mom said, "Take him to the Doctor as soon as you can. Something was not right!" My wife made an appointment for the next day. The Doctor ran a gambit of tests and immediately sent Ryan to the emergency room for more extensive testing. My wife called me at work to inform me of the seriousness of Ryan's condition. I quickly drove to the hospital to be at their side. We were awaiting the results of our son's tests and soon the Doctor came out and told us our son was quite ill. He said his appendix had burst around six days ago and what astonished them was no one lives after six hours in that condition. The Doctor said, in front of Ryan, he should be dead, which frightened Ryan. I immediately came against those words and said, "Ryan, don't accept those words because we know a God, He is a God who heals and brings miracles." Ryan believed the words I spoke to him and peace came to him.

They began to prepare Ryan for exploratory surgery. The Doctor told us to wait and we would be informed of their findings. We immediately went into prayer and prayed to our God of Miracles. We placed our son Ryan in the hands of our God. We waited, hoping for a great report. The Surgeon came out and told us he was amazed. He told us when they opened him up they found two abscesses which had immediately formed when Ryan's appendix ruptured to capture all the poison the appendix poured out. "It was a Miracle", they said. We were extremely relieved at the outcome. My son was now resting after surgery and I knew he would be fine. I had a previously scheduled commitment to minister in Ventura, California so I told my wife I would go and come back the next day. She commented she wasn't happy with my decision to leave under these circumstances but I told her I felt if I took care of God's house then He would take care of ours.

When I got back from ministering I drove back to the hospital to find out my son's white blood count was rising. He also had a high fever. He had an infection somewhere in his body which attributed to his high fever. The Doctors told us they needed to go back in and aspirate and remove a third abscess which was found in another MRI. A total of three abscesses were found in Ryan and the third was the cause of his fever and high white blood count. The second surgery was also a success. He was proclaimed in the hospital as "The Miracle Boy." I thank the Lord for being the God who provides. He provided my son with life.

GOD OF OUR FINANCES

God has shown us His provision is on all facets of our life. He gave us favor with our $1,600,000.00 home to the saving our son. That in itself is more than enough. But, we know a God and He is more than enough. A few months had passed and Ryan was back home with this experience behind him. But, what wasn't behind us, were the bills of the hospital care for Ryan. My wife Loretta received notice we owed

$91,000.00 to the hospital. After the insurance paid their portion we were left with a $56,000.00 balance. Not only did we have that bill to pay but we had many others also.

My wife had all our bills which needed to be paid on the table and she saw we didn't have enough to pay the hospital and the other bills. She decided to forego our tithes to God that week to pay off some other bills and the first installment of the hospital bill. Immediately the Lord spoke audibly to my wife and told her, "Pay my tithes!" She then replied, "I can't, if I pay my tithes then I won't have enough to start paying the hospital!" God again audibly said but with more force, "Pay my tithes first and see what I will do for you!" So my wife wrote out a check for tithes and set it aside and began to write checks for what she was able to pay. She heard the Lord again audibly speak to her saying, "Call the hospital!" "Why am I going to call the hospital? What will I say to them?" The Lord told her, "Request an itemized list of all service and medications rendered." Loretta called and asked for the Accounting Department and requested what the Lord had asked her to do. They put her on hold to search for her information. The accounting clerk returned to the line and questioned my wife and said, "Why does that name sound so familiar? Hold on a second, thats funny I believe I was just working on your account. Mrs. Forniss, you're not going to believe this! I received a call from your insurance company. They are closing out their books for the year. They needed to find a recipient to give a charitable contribution to meet their quota. When they called, I had your file in my hand. When they requested a recipient I told them, why not the Miracle Boy! Mrs. Forniss all you owe is $1,000.00. We're sorry we are unable to remove the $1,000.00 because it is your deductible."

My wife was so appreciative she thanked her profusely and ended the call. She, through eyes filled with tears, thanked the Lord. She realized God was in control and He wanted to have Ryan's miracle extend to our finances. When my wife told me what God did we both were elated and overwhelmed.

You see, God is our provider. He continues to show us He wants to help us in all things. I have learned God always teaches us through diversity and adversity. Every storm we're in offers a God opportunity to mature. Every valley has a test to prove our obedience. Everything we do in Him, through Him, and by Him teaches us He is building us for a greater work. Even in His provision we must learn to hear His instruction, His direction, and our obedience to Him to be at the place of the dispensation of provision.

GOD WHO PROMOTES

I had finished a secular job assignment and was now looking for a new job. I hoped for a new assignment which would promise me a change and a challenge. I was the Senior Pastor of a ministry but couldn't leave my job because the ministry was new and could not yet support me and my family. My resume exemplified my education and extensive managerial experience and skill. At times it was hard to find a job. Many would tell me I was over qualified for the position I was applying for. I went on unemployment while looking for my new assignment. I had been searching for around six months when I came across an ad in the classified section of the Los Angeles Times. It was a job as a collector for a finance company. I called and spoke to the owner of the company. He asked me to fax over my resume, which I did, while he was on the phone with me. He told me the job was a clerk position and they were offering $8.00 an hour. This was in the late 90's. I said to him, "You see my education and work experience, I can be an asset to your company but I need more money." I told him, "I make more money with unemployment than what you are offering." He said, "Sorry, that's the deal I'm offering you. Take it or leave it." I told him, "Thank you so much for your offer, but no thanks." I continued to search all around the Los Angeles and Orange County area but didn't seem to be able to find an assignment that would be a good fit for me.

A week passed and I was pounding the pavement and also driving around to see if maybe I would see a marquee in front of a company which would be advertising job openings. While driving, I looked down at the console of my car, and saw I had a piece of paper with a number written on it and the name of a company. I thought to myself, "Did I call them already?" I couldn't remember but I did see an address on it. I was in the vicinity of that company, so I decided to take a ride there to see what they were offering. I arrived and walked in and asked if I could speak to the manager or owner of the company. I also asked if they had a job opening and the receptionist replied, "Yes." A tall, thin, middle-aged man came out and introduced himself and asked me to have a seat. I told him my name was Al Forniss and I was inquiring about the job opening. He said, "Wait, why do I know you? Didn't you call me last week? Aren't you the guy I spoke to and said you were over qualified and you would be bored with being a bill collector?" I was so embarrassed and I didn't want to tell him I made a mistake and I didn't want the job. It must have been pride because God knows our heart and knew at that time I would not admit to this mistake. Help me Lord. I told him, "Yes, I am the same man who spoke to you on the phone but I thought you might reconsider hiring me. If you can maybe give me just a little more money we can negotiate or something." He said, "Listen you came in here and you knew it was $8.00 an hour I had offered. If you want this job, it's yours but don't complain later it's not challenging enough for you." I asked again, "What about at least $10.00 an hour?" He said, "No, $8.00." God spoke to me and said, "Take this job offer and see what I will do for you." I was thinking, as he waited for my answer, my wife might be upset bringing home less money with this job than unemployment. I looked at him and said, "Yes, I'll take it. When do you want me to start?" "Tomorrow, but are you sure?", He asked.

I went home to tell my wife about my new position. I made sure to tell her first God told me to take it and He was going to do something with me there. She told me if God told you, you have to take it. He will provide for us. He always does.

In the morning I went to work and sat at my new desk. They gave me a tour of the office and explained my duties. My new employer told another worker to introduce me to the programs and work schedule. He gave both me and the woman across from me a three page list of 150 customers who were 30,60,90, and even 120 days delinquent. He said, "Call each one and see if you can get promises or payments." I said to Him, "No worries I'll do the best I can!" He said, "Have you ever collected before?" "No, but I can learn."

During the day he would pass my desk and peek to see the progress. I would smile at him and give him the thumbs up and he would just shake his head. At the end of the day he came to me and said, "It's been about six hours since you have been working on the list and you're still on the middle of the first page?" I said, "What do you mean? I finished all the list and I am now going back to review them." "You have to be kidding me!" He replied. He asked the woman who was working on her list how much progress had she made? She replied, "Oh about maybe half the list." He looked at me and said, "She has been here quite a long time with me and is one of our best collectors. You're still on the first page. I'm sure you have done a good job but you are too slow. You are costing me money. I don't think you're going to work out." "Listen, I have worked all the pages, the whole list and now I'm rechecking my work." "You mean you've called all those customers? Every single one of them?" "Yes." "Can't be done, Al. Okay, let me see," while pointing to one of the customers on the first page. "Bring that one up on the computer." I did and I said, "See here I wrote, spoke to Jane and asked her what was the problem of her not being able to pay. We resolved the issue and she is coming in tomorrow by three o'clock to bring her account up-to-date." Next he pointed to a customer at the bottom of the second page and I looked him up and said, "He gave me his credit card. He paid for one month and also paid for an extension. He is now up-to-date." He went to the last page and realized that I, had in fact, worked them all with great success. He congratulated me and said he was sorry and realized he found a diamond in me.

My first month there was a month of change in the company. They were changing to a new software and converting their collection department procedures to a complete new system. The owners asked me if I would go with the head of each department to learn how to implement the new system. I said, "Absolutely." We arrived at the Software Company and were greeted and guided into a classroom. They began to share with us how their system worked and how to install it. It was an all-day training seminar. We knew because we were going to shut down our system we needed to find the most efficient way to bring up the new system as quickly as possible. We finished the classed and headed back to our company.

The day of our conversion was at hand. I was not the head of any department and I knew it was not my responsibility to prepare or to coordinate this project. I stayed back and did all I could do to keep my desk running. When they began to program and input all the parameters necessary to allow the new system to run they couldn't remember the procedure which had to be taken to efficiently transition smoothly. It took quite a few hours for the owners to realize the managers and lead employees were either not remembering what was taught at the seminar or they had no experience necessary to be of help. The owner was upset and told everyone to just stop what they were doing and go back to their desks. He came to me and asked if I remembered the procedure we were taught at the seminar? I said, "I believe so." "Can you help me?" He asked. "Well, I will try but you must give me the authorization to override each department head and to have them listen to my instructions allowing me to fully direct the transition." He replied, "Al, if you could do this that would be a miracle."

I went to each department and sat each person down and reviewed the task at hand. Next I went into the back office of each program and reprogrammed them. I taught each department how to use the new system dependent on their work need. At the end of the day every employee and department were now working with our new system and all was running smoothly. The owner thanked me and was pleased. I thanked him and went back to work collecting.

A month passed and I was still teaching and helping many of the employees learn the system. I was also getting many calls from other outside companies who had purchased the same system. They wanted to ask what I thought of the system and would eventually ask if I knew how to implement this or that. I would help them but didn't know word would get around the industry because many were calling me for help rather than the Software Company. I received a phone call from the Software Company offering me a job with them as their Director of Customer Service. I told them I would let them know. There offer was very generous and much more than what I was making. I asked the owner if I would be able to speak with him and he said, "Absolutely, how may I help you, Al?" I told him I was giving him my two weeks' notice because another company had offered me a job I could not refuse. I am not telling you this, so we can negotiate a pay raise or promotion but only to inform you as a courtesy. He said, "You're not being fair. What do you mean? Can't you at least give us a try to keep you, please? What do you want for me to say? Just give me twenty-four hours and I'll get back to you with our offer." I told him I would.

I came to work the next day and was greeted by the owner. "Al, please come with me. I want you to stay with us. Since you have been here the company has seen great changes. There is something about you which is different. You bring out the best in all of us. I want to promote you to General Manager of the finance company, a pay raise from $8.00 an hour to $18.50. I want to give you three weeks' vacation starting immediately. I also want to give you $1,000.00 in cash for my appreciation in what you have already done for my company. If you take the offer or not I want you to keep the money, you've earned it. Come on, please just say yes!" I looked at him and said, "I will stay." We both hugged and walked back in. Can you imagine, I walked out with him as a collector and walked back in as his General Manager? Only God!

God was teaching me to trust Him. I was bringing home more money on unemployment than what the company was paying me, but God spoke and said, "Take the job and see what I am going to do." God blessed me in many different ways as I became obedient to Him. My first act of obedience was my tithes to God. This act placed me in the position to receive. But, what did I receive? I received divine favor, divine knowledge, divine understanding, divine promotion, divine provision. What more could I have asked for?

I have found the key to God's success in provision. God is obligated to bless you and provide for you, because the word of God is true and cannot turn back void. He tells us in Malachi 3:10-12 *"Bring the whole tithe into the storehouse, that there may be food in my house. Test me in this, says the Lord Almighty, and see if I will not throw open the floodgates of heaven and pour out so much blessing that you will not have room enough for it. I will prevent pest from devouring your crops and the vines in your fields will not cast their fruit, says the Lord Almighty. Then all the nations will call you blessed for yours will be a delightful land, says the Lord Almighty."*

The Lord tells us He is not a respecter of persons in Acts 10:34. God loves you as He does me. You can have all your needs met but also your desires. If you are going through some rough times and seem not to be able to come out of them, find a church (store house) and give your tithes and offerings to Him. Watch and see God too will position you to receive to the point of pressed down, shaken together, and running over. (Luke 6:38). You can't out give God. He is Jehovah Jireh the God of provision. Test Him today and see your tomorrow breakthrough for you.

Dear Reader,

When the Lord placed in me to write a book it became a dream nestled deep inside my heart but never believing in a million years it would one day become a reality. I thought He wanted me to write an autobiography, sharing my personal life from the beginning. But He told me this book would be completely different to what I had imagined. The Lord wanted me to share my experiences I had with Him.

I received many prophetic words throughout the years, I would author books which would touch millions of lives and draw them closer to the Lord. I decided to begin this book and for three days I sat in front of my laptop struggling because I didn't know how to start. It was as if I had "Writer's Block". At the end of the third day the Lord spoke to me and said, "Share what I have taught you through my encounters, visitations and miracles I have had with you. Let them know I am the same God of yesterday, today, and forever. Let them know I love them. Let them see you know a God! Show them I am alive in you and in them." I said, "Yes Lord, I will do as you ask. Please allow the Holy Spirit to guide me in the way you would have this book to be authored."

This is exactly what I have done. I pray my visitations, my encounters, and stories with the Lord, will draw you closer to Him. I ask, from the bottom of my heart, you give Jesus a chance to show you He is real. I personally am not concerned what religion you are following. I am not concerned of your ethnicity, or your economic status only your Salvation. Jesus is not about religion. Religion has been the inception of every war known to man. Jesus is only about relationship, yours and His. I am not here to change your religion but to compliment where you are with Jesus becoming your Lord and Savior.

If you have been blessed and moved by my experiences with the Lord, I challenge you to seek Him for yourself. Ask the Lord to forgive your sins and invite Him in your heart to be your Lord and Savior. Do this in the name of Jesus. If what I am asking you to do for yourself is false, you have not lost anything. But, If I am right, you will gain everything.

May God bless you and keep you. I pray peace, health, and prosperity be yours in abundance.

In the love of the Lord,
Apostle Dr Al G Forniss

ABOUT THE AUTHOR

Apostle Dr. Al G. Forniss is the founder of Theophany Ministries, International. He serves as their Apostle and Senior Pastor. For over 30 years he has traveled and preached the Gospel of Jesus Christ. He is known for his accomplished and highly anointed voice in song. He is a powerfully gifted international orator. Due to his Apostolic mantle and God given gifts of Miracles and Healing since the age of fourteen, he continues to hold powerful Miracle Crusades all over the world where signs and wonders follow. He is sought out globally. He has been married to his childhood sweetheart, Loretta for 43 years and they are blessed with three sons, three daughters-in-love and six beautiful grandchildren. He has received many awards and acknowledgements for his accomplishments. Amongst them, The U.S. Congressional House of Representatives Award was given to him for his outstanding and invaluable service to humanity, He was also awarded Israel's Peace Award. Dr. Forniss holds an Honorary Doctorate of Divinity and a Doctorate of Healing from California State Christian University. He recently became the recipient of a Masters of Theology from Theophany School of Ministry

Contact Information:

email: ApostleAl@tmichurch.org
951-734-4707
P.O. Box 5747
Norco, California 92860

Made in the USA
San Bernardino, CA
03 January 2017